AMERICA
SIMPLIFIED

What You Need to Know

For ages 8+, new Americans, Visitors, and Tourists

Written by MICHAEL NTABAAZI

HARD COVER: ISBN-13: 978-1-7330819-2-4

PAPERBACK: ISBN-13: 978-1-7330819-0-0

EBOOK: ISBN-13: 978-1-7330819-1-7

Library of Congress Control Number: 2019905336

This is a work of creative nonfiction. Some parts have been fictionalized in varying degrees, for various purposes. There is no chronological order of some events. For the fictitious parts, any resemblance to actual persons, living or dead, events or locales is entirely coincidental. Except for archive images which are a property of the author, all images and illustrations in the book have been permitted for use courtesy of their owners who have been acknowledged in the book and also in the bibliography where their websites or affiliated websites have been sited. Included in the book too are images that are freely available in the public domain.

Front and Back cover image by : Author.
Book edited by: bookhelpline.com
North Dakota symbol illustration by : Tom Kelly.
Book illustration by : Author.
Printed by: Amazon Kindle Direct Publishing (KDP)
Ebook by : Amazon (Kindle Direct Publishing) KDP.

First printing edition 2019.

Publisher: Michael Ntabaazi
14 Greenview Street, #114
 Framingham, MA , 01701
E-mail: micangel71@gmail.com

AMERICA SIMPLIFIED

What You Need to Know

Book Author: Michael Ntabaazi

DEDICATION

To Jedd, my son.

I hope this book will be fun to read and help you learn new things.

PREFACE

This book has been written to make it easy for students and "new Americans" to learn and get a handle on the essentials of the United States of America. The aim is to pass on the history, culture and life-style of America in a simplified and humorous way, making sure that what is read and learnt here forms lasting impressions on the lives of the readers. For the new American, visitor, and tourist, this book combines everything you need to know about this country.

Many books out there—whether fiction or non-fiction—dedicated to children or not—have been written on various topics including science, history, and geography, but I have yet to see a book that sums up what this great continent and country is all about in a simplified version that appeals to both students and new Americans including visitors to this country.

I have had an opportunity to interact with many children of my friends including my own son at the elementary school level as a parent, but I was shocked to learn that some children don't even know the name of the state where they live or the capital city of the United States of America. To know the Founding Fathers of the United States or to be asked how many years the United States has been independent could make many a student or visitor scratch their heads in search of answers. It is therefore the hope of this author that this book will be the first of its kind to address such a missing link in the lives of these students and equip them with much needed information in these early stages of life. In doing so, students will grow up well-informed about their country and surrounding neighborhood, encouraging patriotism from an early age, thus putting them in a better position to contribute effectively to nation building.

For those aspiring to become citizens of the United States, this book has information that will help you answer some of the civic and naturalization test questions that are asked at the interview process an applicant must pass before becoming a citizen; and to the visitors, this book is a one-stop center to being grounded in the American way of life.

Signed: Michael Ntabaazi

Framingham MA, U.S.A

8/13/2018

ACKNOWLEDGEMENT

I would like to pay special tribute to Dr. Festo Lugolobi, my loyal friend, author, professor, educator, and entrepreneur who challenged me to think deeply about how I can make a difference in my life and the lives of those around me. Without his challenges in times when I faced difficulty, I would not have been able to write this book. Thank you Dr. Lugolobi for believing in me.

Secondly, special thanks to Nevin Mays, an editor from Portland, Oregon, U.S.A who is listed on reedsy.com , a website for authors, editors, and writers. Her constructive critique and advice about my book made me revisit parts of it to make it more robust, appealing, and appropriate for my intended audience.

To all my friends who supported me during this new and challenging phase in my life, I say to you, "thank you very much".

INTRODUCTION

AMERICA SIMPLIFIED: **What You Need To Know** is a visual book that sums up life in the United States of America. The book is divided into sections which explain the core values and symbols of the United States, the federal and state governments, American people and culture, life expectancy and quality of life, inventions and discoveries, plus a look at how the world views America and, in turn, how the United States views other countries.

It is the intention of the author to focus on the above topics and subjects because they summarize the majority of the life experiences of America and its peoples. To produce a book of this kind, the author spent many months scouring the internet and reviewing articles, annual reports, and blogs from news and corporate organization websites for material relevant to the book. Much of this material was scattered all over the internet and no single book contained what the author was looking for. It was the task of the author to gather and put together this material with corresponding images and visuals. This was not an easy venture to embark upon; from the selection process of what to include, to the determination of whether what was included would be relevant and of value to the learning experience of both a young and adult reader.

To make sure that the content of the book is relevant to readers, the author whose background and professional life was in the print and broadcast media , engaged and interacted with a number of Americans of all age groups, who through interviews about the book's topics and subjects, expressed a great ignorance about the state of affairs in their states, and worse still, very little knowledge about the issues that have made America stand out. From these interactions, the author was assured that the contents of the book would remain relevant, essential and vital to the reading and learning needs of a wide section of people in the United States. The employment of visuals in the book is meant to make it easy for readers to have a mental picture of what the author is writing about and to encourage them to visit those locations and sites that stand out and make lasting impressions.

This book consists of eleven chapters rich with photos, tables, illustrations, and maps of the rich and diverse culture and life-style that America has to offer. The author makes a deliberate effort to compare demographics within the United States and to those of other countries, showcasing the attractions that pull other countries and peoples to the U.S.

America Simplified is a book based on facts and these facts present the country as it is today with a shade of its past, and takes pride in those aspects that continue to make this nation a great one. Whoever reads this book will surely walk away more informed than they were before. To the children of this great country, I hope the knowledge acquired will become the building blocks to a solid foundation in their education and civic life to come.,

TABLE OF CONTENT

1

FACTS ABOUT THE UNITED STATES OF AMERICA

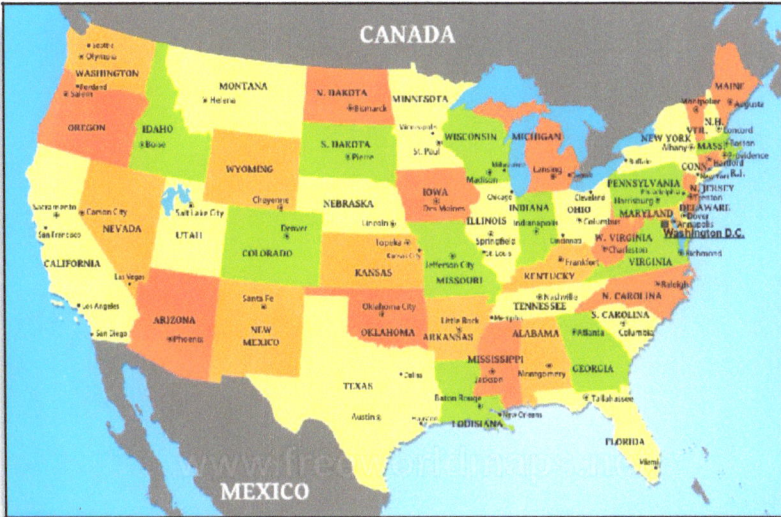

Map of the U.S.A
Source: http://www.freeworldmaps.net

Did you know that the very first plane was invented in the United States?

Yes, the first aircraft was invented by the Wright Brothers (Wilbur and Orville Wright of Dayton, Ohio) in 1903.

If that seemed like an easy one to get, how about this: What do the following presidents of the United States of America have in common? Franklin Pierce, John F. Kennedy, Bill Clinton.

The answer to this question and many others to blow your mind and keep you on edge can be found in the pages ahead.

Location of U.S.A

LOCATION

The United States shares its border with Canada in the North, the Atlantic Ocean in the East, Mexico and the Gulf of Mexico in the South, and the Pacific Ocean in the West. It is located in the western hemisphere on the continent of North America.

The U.S. is the third or fourth largest country in the world and its total area including Alaska and Hawaii is 9.8 million square kilometers (or 3.8 million square miles) according to the CIA world fact book. Both the United Nations Statistics Division and Encyclopedia Britannica give varying figures depending on whether they include the total area of the Great Lakes waters and coastal waters or not. This inclusion or omission of the total area of the Great Lakes waters and coastal waters in the total area of the United States, is the determinant of whether the U.S. is the third or fourth largest country in the world.

Source: https://en.wikipedia.org/wiki/Geography_of_the_United_States

CLIMATE

Now that you know where the United States of America is located and about the large masses of land and water surrounding the country, you might be wondering what impact this has on the continent when it comes to climate change.

The news from time to time of huge wild fires burning in the western state of California, and the year round hurricanes and tornadoes spread all over the United States—not to forget the severe weather that disrupts schools, states, and federal government activities during the winter and summer seasons— would make anyone want to get acquainted with the climate and weather patterns in this country.

Besides, if you are the travelling type or intend to visit and/or study in the United States, knowledge of U.S. climate and weather conditions, including the changing seasons, will help you decide where to go, what type of clothes to carry, what to buy or not, and the mental and physical preparation you will need to meet any challenges along the way.

Below is the breakdown of climate in the United States:

Climate in the U.S. varies from region to region and is influenced by differences in the angular distance (latitude) North or South of the equator. Mountains and deserts have also contributed to changes in climate and weather.

- ❖ To cut a long story short about this climate phenomenon, when you move West of the 100th meridian (an imaginary line running from the north to south pole) through the United States, the conditions are semi-arid to desert like. This covers the southwestern U.S.
  - ➢ The coast of California experiences a Mediterranean type of climate. This makes summers very hot and quite dry in the Southwestern and West region, while East of the imaginary line the summers are hot and humid.
- ❖ The region East of the 100th meridian covers the Northern areas, East through New England (where the climate is humid continental), and the plains and southern states of America (where the climate is humid subtropical).
- ❖ Southern Florida is tropical as well as Hawaii and the U.S. Virgin Islands.
- ❖ The Rocky Mountains and Sierra Nevada are alpine (average weather conditions for regions above the tree line—or, simply put—conditions that cause trees to fail to grow due to cold), while the west coast of Washington State and Oregon have an oceanic type of climate.
- ❖ Alaska is largely sub-arctic (long, usually very cold winters, and short, cool to mild summers) although it has a sub-polar oce-

anic climate (generally cool summers and cool winters) in the Southeast and Southwestern parts of the state.

Phew, that was not easy to take in but luckily its behind us now and I hope you are catching up with me.

THE NATIONAL ANTHEM

The National Anthem of the United States of America is "The Star-Spangled Banner".

The lyrics or words come from "Defense of Fort M'Henry," a poem written by Francis Scott Key— at that time a 35 year-old lawyer and amateur poet—on September 14, 1814. Francis Scott Key wrote the poem after witnessing the bombardment of Fort McHenry by the British ships of the Royal Navy in Baltimore Harbor. This was during the Battle of Baltimore in the war of 1812.

Francis Scott Key was inspired by the U.S. victory and the sight of the United States flag that was flying triumphantly above the fort after the war. The flag with fifteen stars and stripes had been made by Mary Young Pickersgill, the daughter of another notable flag maker, Rebbecca Young Pickersgill in Baltimore.

The poem, according to the free encyclopedia Wikipedia, was set to the tune of a popular British song "To Anacreon in Heaven" or "The Anacreontic Song", written by John Stafford Smith for the Anacreontic Society, which was a men's popular club of amateur musicians in London in the mid-18th century.

Set to Key's poem, and renamed "The Star-Spangled Banner", it soon became a popular patriotic song. The "Star-Spangled Banner", was recognized for official use by the United States Navy in 1889, and by the U.S. President Woodrow Wilson in 1916 when he ordered for the song to be played at military and other appropriate occasions. The "Star-Spangled Banner" became the official national anthem of the U.S. in 1931 after the House of Representatives and the Senate passed the bill on March 3, 1931 and signed into law the following day by President Herbert Hoover, on March 4,1931. Prior to the signing of the bill, the Veterans of Foreign Wars had started a petition in 1930 for the United States to officially recognize the "Star-Spangled Banner" as the national anthem. This petition was signed later by 5 million people in favor.

It should be noted, however, that before 1931, there were other songs which served as the   official hymns of the United States. These included "Hail Columbia" (a patriotic song which is the ceremonial entrance march of the Vice President of the U.S.), which served for most of the 19th century, "My Country, T's of Thee" (also known as 'America') another patriotic American song with the same melody as the national anthem of the United Kingdom "God Save the Queen". This song served as the actual (de facto) national anthem of the U.S. following the war of 1812 and other subsequent wars. "America the Beautiful", is another of those popular patriotic songs that competed for recognition at popular events.

There were several versions of the "Star-Spangled Banner" by the early 20th century. In an effort to find one singular version, President Woodrow Wilson who served as the 28th President of the United States from 1913-1921, charged the U.S. Bureau of Education the responsibility of the task. After enlisting five musicians, the standardized version of the song was voted on by these musicians and it premiered at the Carnegie Hall in New York on December 5, 1917.

Source: https://en.wikipedia.org/wiki/The_Star-Spangled_Banner

Image of the "Star Spangled Banner"
Source: https://www.loc.gov/resource/ihas.100010134.0/?sp=2

Image of Francis Scott Key
Source: https://en.wikipedia.org/wiki/Francis_Scott_Key

THE FLAG

Like many symbols, the flag of the United States is an identity element that unites all Americans and gives them a sense of pride and belonging. It evokes strong feelings of patriotism and when hoisted outside the borders of the country, it reminds citizens where they come from and cements the collective responsibility they have to one another especially in times of distress.

The flag is also a reminder to friends and foes of the sovereignty of the United States like any other country, and of the influence it holds globally. Seen from near or far, the U.S. flag has an ability to bring up a lot of good memories unlike any other U.S. symbol. No wonder, some artists have composed songs about the flag and used the pattern of the flag itself to make souvenirs, placards, postcards, caps, and whatever else comes to your mind. This occurs because of the special importance they attach to the flag in their personal lives— their sense of nationalism as it were.

U.S Flag

Photo Source: https://images.pexels.com/photos/457563/pexels-photo-457563.jpeg?auto=compress&cs=tinysrgb&dpr=2&h=650&w=940

The flag has 13 horizontal stripes of red and white, and a blue rectangle in the canton (or the "union"). The union bears fifty white, five pointed stars which represent the 50 States of the U.S.A.

The Colors of The National Flag

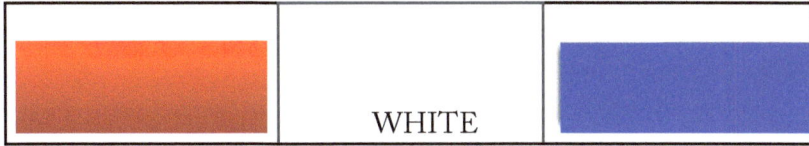

WHITE

Meaning of the Colors

The colors red, white, and blue did not hold any particular meaning for the stars and stripes when it was adopted in 1777. This is according to a book Our Flag published in 1989 by the House of Representatives. The practice by some writers and orators of giving meaning to the colors of the flag is therefore in error according to the above book, Our Flag.

However, the colors in the Great Seal (a unique symbol of the U.S. on which the front side or obverse bears the coat of arms) have specific meaning: The colors of the pales (the vertical stripes) are those used in the flag of the USA. White signifies purity and innocence; Red signifies hardiness and valor; Blue is the color of the chief (the broad band above the stripes) and signifies vigilance, perseverance, and justice.

THE GREAT SEAL

Note: The mission to devise a seal for the United States of America reflecting the Founding Father's beliefs, values, and the sovereignty of the New Nation, became a reality on June 20, 1782. The 13 stripes represent the thirteen Colonies that declared independence from Great Britain in 1776. These colonies became the first states in the U.S.

Source: https://www.britannica.com/topic/flag-of-the-United-States-of-America, http://www.usflag.org/colors.html

It is said that no one knows with absolute certainty the person who designed or for that matter made the first stars and stripes, but most historians believe it was Congressman **Francis Hopkinson,** a popular patriot and lawyer from New Jersey, U.S.A. This Congressman was one of the signatories to the Declaration of Independence. The decision to have an official flag of the new nation was made by the Continental Congress when on June 14, 1777 it passed the **First Flag Act:** "Resolved, That the flag of the United States be made of thirteen stripes, alternate red and white; that the union be thirteen stars, white in a blue field, representing a new Constellation."

Subsequent acts and executive orders were made, changing the design and composition of the stripes and stars and their arrangement. The stars and stripes were increased from thirteen to fifteen in 1795 when Vermont and Kentucky joined the union as states. It was the fifteen stars and fifteen stripes flag that inspired Francis Scott Key to write the poem "Defense of Fort M'Henry", that became the "Star-Spangled Banner".

On April 4, 1818, Congress passed a plan that changed the number of stars on the flag from 15 to 20. In the plan, a new star would be added to the flag each time a new state was admitted to the union. However, the number of stripes were reduced from fifteen to the original thirteen to honor the original colonies. The act also specified that new designs of the flag would officially take effect on the first July 4 (Independence Day) following the admission of one or more new states.

The most recent change from 49 stars to 50 happened in 1960 when Hawaii gained statehood in August 1959.

Source : https://en.wikipedia.org/wiki/Flag_of_the_United_States, http://www.usflag.org/history/flagevolution.html,
http://www.usflag.org/colors.html

I

Do you remember the question I posed at the beginning of this section about the similarities of three past U.S. Presidents? Well, if you have not already come up with the answer, here it is: President Franklin Pierce, John F. Kennedy, and Bill Clinton fall into the category of "Most Handsome Presidents of the U.S." According to the "hottest heads of state" website https://hottestheadsofstate.com/us-presidents/ dedicated to carrying out polls and seeking public opinion on anything and everything , president Franklin Pierce, who governed from 1853-1857 and died in 1869, is the most handsome of them all. He is said to have been gorgeous, charming, polite, thoughtful and popular.

Below is a list of the 10 most handsome U.S. presidents. You can disagree with what is here or put up your own list, but hey, isn't this an interesting subject regardless?

1. Franklin Pierce (1853-1857) Democrat.
2. James K. Polk (1845-1849) Democrat.
3. John F. Kennedy (1961-1963) Democrat. A.K.A JFK. He was the second youngest president (aged 43) ever to be elected after Theodore Roosevelt. He was also the only Catholic President.
4. Theodore Roosevelt (1901-1909) Republican. It is said someone tried to assassinate Roosevelt by shooting him in the chest, but he survived because his chest was too heavily muscled for the bullet to pass through, and thereafter he went to give a campaign speech! Awesome hunk!
5. Ulysses S. Grant (1869-1877) Republican.
6. Barak Obama (2009-2017) Democrat. He is the first African American U.S. President. His presidency saw the passing and enactment of a national health-care act which came to be known as "Obama Care".

7. James A. Garfield (March 4, 1881-September 19, 1881) Republican. He was assassinated after 200 days in office.
8. George W. Bush (2001-2009) Republican. His presidency saw the longest post-World War II recession in 2007.
9. Franklin D. Roosevelt (1933-1945) Democrat. A.K.A FDR. He is consistently regarded by scholars as one of the top three U.S. Presidents. He was the only U.S. President to serve three terms.., after which an amendment was drafted that declared the two-term limit in the U.S. Constitution.
10. Thomas Jefferson (1801-1809) Democratic-Republican. One of the Founding Fathers of the U.S. and author of the Declaration of Independence. It is said he wished America to become an "empire of liberty" representing the ideals of republicanism.

N.B: (Please pay attention to this) Stay with me because this is just getting started.

THE NATIONAL EMBLEM

Bald Eagle

The Bald Eagle was chosen in June 20, 1782 as the emblem of the U.S. due to its long life, great strength, and majestic looks. It was also believed then that it existed only in the United States. However, the Bald Eagle is found also in Canada.

Where can we see the Bald Eagle? On the backs of U.S gold coins, the silver dollar, the half dollar, and the quarter. Also, the Bald Eagle with spread wings can be seen on the Great Seal.

Facts about the Bald Eagle

- The Latin name of the Bald Eagle is Haliaeetus Leucocephalus which means white headed sea eagle.

- The Bald Eagle is Alaska's largest resident bird of prey and there are more Bald Eagles in that state than anywhere else in the U.S.

- The Bald Eagle is the spiritual symbol of the Alaska Natives for hundreds of years before the bird was even chosen as the emblem of the U.S.

- The bird is called "bald "or "balled" not because it is a hairless bird, but because the word was used in those early times to mean white or white-faced.

- Adult Bald Eagles have a dark brown body, a white head and tail, yellow feet, a beak, and eyes.

- Immature eagles normally have a dark brown body, showing white in the wing linings and breast. The head, tail, beak, and eyes are brown, but it is similar in appearance to the golden eagle without white on the tail.

- Bald Eagles have bare legs whereas golden eagles have feathered legs to the toes.

- The Bald Eagle has a snowy white head and tail feathers and its wings are straight in addition to its large size. Body weights of Bald Eagles range from 3.6 to 6.4 kilograms (8 to 14 pounds).

- The Bald Eagle used to be an endangered species but no longer according to the Eagle Nature Foundation website. Only the Southwestern Bald Eagles are still on the endangered list.

- There are no Bald Eagles in Hawaii.

Source: http://eaglenature.com/eagle_facts.php,

http://www.adfg.alaska.gov/index.cfm?adfg=baldeagle.main

HEAD OF FEDERAL GOVERNMENT

The head of the federal government is the president. The president is also the head of state and commander in chief of the armed forces of the United States of America. Under article II of the U.S. Constitution, the president is responsible for the execution and enforcement of the laws created by Congress.

- ❖ The president appoints heads of federal agencies like the Department of Defense and the cabinet. The cabinet and independent federal agencies are responsible for the day-to-day implementation and administration of federal laws.

- ❖ The Vice-President is also part of the Executive Branch and is on stand-by to take over the duties and responsibilities of the president should the need arise.

❖ The president has the power to sign acts, bills, or statutes into law and to veto bills enacted by congress. However, the congress can override a rejection by the president to sign a bill into law with a two-thirds vote of both houses.

❖ The president and executive branch carry out diplomacy initiatives with other countries and the president has the power to negotiate and sign treaties, which must be ratified by two-thirds of the Senate.

❖ The president has unlimited power to pardon and set free any citizen who has committed a federal crime; the only exception is if that person is under impeachment proceedings.

❖ It is a constitutional requirement for the president of the United States to from time to time give Congress information on the State of the Union and recommend for their consideration such measures as he/she might judge necessary.

❖ To become president of the United States, the constitution lists only three things which are: One must be 35 years of age, a natural born citizen, and must have lived in the United States for 14 years.

❖ The president is elected every four years and is limited to two four-year terms.

❖ Interestingly, the president of the United States is not in fact elected by the people but by members of the Electoral College. These people are elected by the population on the first Tuesday of November in the fourth year. The electors represent each member of their congressional delegation from the 50 states. Presently, there are 538 electors in the Electoral College. These are the ones who cast their votes for the president.

Source: https://www.whitehouse.gov/about-the-white-house/the-exe-cutive-branch/

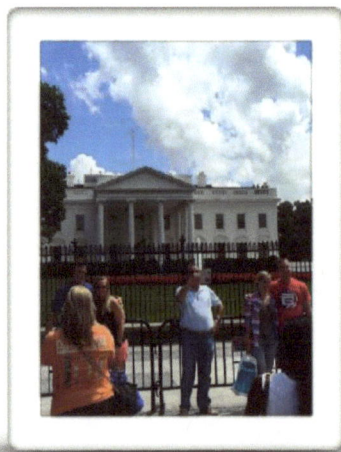

The White House

THE CURRENCY

The currency (or money) used in the United States is the Dollar ($), code USD, and also abbreviated as US$. The use of the U.S. Dollar first began in 1792. The currency is divided into 100 smaller cent (¢) units.

The frequently used coins are in the denominations of 1¢, 5¢, 10¢, and 25¢.

50¢, and $1 coins are rarely used. The bank notes frequently used are $1, $5, $10, $20, $50, and $100. $2 bills are rarely used. Source: https://en.wikipedia.org/wiki/United_States_dollar

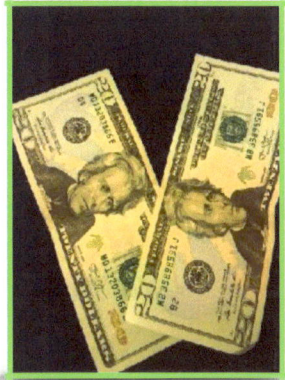

U.S. Currency (Archive photos).

2

THE COUNTRY

North America is the third largest continent of the seven continents of the world.

The United States is made up of 50 States, with Washington, D.C being the capital of the United States of America. Washington D.C is a small city on the Potomac River that borders the States of Maryland and Virginia.

The United States of America was declared a new nation on July 4, 1776, independent from the British Empire. The fourth of July is Independence Day in the U.S. On that day in 1776, the United States of America had 13 Colonies (unlike the 50 States we have today), which broke away from the rule of Great Britain when the Second Continental Congress voted and declared independence on July 4.

The American colonists were citizens of Great Britain and subjects of King George III, the English monarch of the time. The American colonists broke away from their mother land due to trade restrictions (the colonists relied on Great Britain for imported supplies and trade was restricted due to a limited supply of money and no banks) and imposition of several taxes (like the Stamp Act of 1765 which required the use of a special paper bearing an embossed tax stamp for all legal documents and the Townsend Acts of 1767 which required the colonists to pay taxes on imported goods like tea) which they saw as unfair and unconstitutional.

The above taxes were imposed by the British government to pay for its war debts in the French Indian war that ended in 1763 and also required for the colonists to pay for the lodging of British Soldiers stationed in America through the Quartering Act of 1765.

The colonists felt they should not pay these taxes because they were passed in England by parliament and not by their own colonial governments. Further still, they saw no need for soldiers to be stationed in the colonies after the end of the French Indian war. The colonists said these taxes violated their rights as British citizens.

The protests that ensued led to the boycott or refusal to buy British goods. This led to actions like the Boston Tea Party in 1773 where colonists dressed up like Indians, sneaked onto ships in the Boston harbor, and dumped the imported tea into the water, as well as battles fought in 1775 in Lexington and Concord Massachusetts between colonists and the British Army.

Opposition to British coercive rule and its increasing military presence in the colonies led to the first and second Continental Congress where the American colonists eventually declared independence from British rule, realizing that King George III had declared the colonies in rebellion on August 23, 1775 and that he had no intention of reconciling with them or removing the ministers responsible for the repressive legislation.

Source: https://www.historyisfun.org/pdf/tea-overboard/Why_were_the_American_colonies_unhappy_with_the_British_government.pdf , http://www.history.org/almanack/life/politics/4thjuly.cfm , https://www.history.com/this-day-in-history/american-colonies-declare-independence

THE STATES

The 50 U.S. states, in alphabetical order are:

1.	Alabama	10.	Georgia	19.	Maine
2.	Alaska	11.	Hawaii	20.	Maryland
3.	Arizona	12.	Idaho	21.	Massachusetts
4.	Arkansas	13.	Illinois	22.	Michigan
5.	California	14.	Indiana	23.	Minnesota
6.	Colorado	15.	Iowa	24.	Mississippi
7.	Connecticut	16.	Kansas	25.	Missouri
8.	Delaware	17.	Kentucky	26.	Montana
9.	Florida	18.	Louisiana	27.	Nebraska

28.	Nevada	36.	Oklahoma	44.	Utah
29.	New Hampshire	37.	Oregon	45.	Vermont
30.	New Jersey	38.	Pennsylvania	46.	Virginia
31.	New Mexico	39.	Rhode Island	47.	Washington
32.	New York	40.	South Carolina	48.	West Virginia
33.	North Carolina	41.	South Dakota	49.	Wisconsin
34.	North Dakota	42.	Tennessee	50.	Wyoming
35.	Ohio	43.	Texas		

Note: Wyoming is the smallest U.S. state in human population, while California is the largest in human population. Rhode Island is the smallest U.S. state in size, while Alaska is largest in size.

CAPITALS OF THE 50 US STATES

U.S. STATES		CAPITAL CITIES	U.S. STATES		CAPITAL CITIES
1.	Alabama	Montgomery	9.	Florida	Tallahassee
2.	Alaska	Juneau	10.	Georgia	Atlanta
3.	Arizona	Phoenix	11.	Hawaii	Honolulu
4.	Arkansas	Little Rock	12.	Idaho	Boise
5.	California	Sacramento	13.	Illinois	Springfield
6.	Colorado	Denver	14.	Indiana	Indianapolis
7.	Connecticut	Hartford	15.	Iowa	Des Moines
8.	Delaware	Dover	16.	Kansas	Topeka

U.S. STATES	CAPITAL CITIES	U.S. STATES	CAPITAL CITIES
17. Kentucky	Frankfort	30. New Jersey	Trenton
18. Louisiana	Baton Rouge	31. New Mexico	Santa Fe
19. Maine	Augusta	32. New York	Albany
20. Maryland	Annapolis	33. North Carolina	Raleigh
21. Massachu-setts	Boston	34. North Dakota	Bismark
22. Michigan	Lansing	35. Ohio	Columbus
23. Minnesota	St. Paul	36. Oklahoma	Oklahoma City
24. Mississippi	Jackson	37. Oregon	Salem
25. Missouri	Jefferson City	38. Pennsylva-nia	Harrisburg
26. Montana	Helena	39. Rhode Island	Providence
27. Nebraska	Lincoln	40. South Carolina	Columbia
28. Nevada	Carson City	41. South Dakota	Pierre
29. New Hampshire	Concord	42. Tennessee	Nashville

43.	Texas	Austin	47.	Washington	Olympia	
44.	Utah	Salt Lake City	48.	West Virginia	Charleston	
45.	Vermont	Montpelier	49.	Wisconsin	Madison	
46.	Virginia	Richmond	50.	Wyoming	Cheyenne	

SYMBOLS OF THE 50 U.S. STATES

State symbols represent the cultural heritage and natural treasures of each state. States have many official symbols, but for purposes of this book, only one symbol will be mentioned from each state. Images are provided where legally possible.

STATE	SYMBOL	IMAGE
1. Alabama	The Seal of Alabama (1876) Alabama has 41 official state emblems. The oldest of which is the Alabama State Bible from 1853 and the most recent being the Peach, Alabama's State fruit tree (2006).	Public Domain Use https://commons.wikimedia.org/wiki/File:Seal_of_Alabama.svg
2. Alaska	The North Star and the Big Dipper on a field of blue (1927) Alaska has 17 State emblems.	Public Domain Image On https://upload.wikimedia.org/wikipedia/commons/thumb/e/e6/Flag_of_Alaska.svg/1600px-Flag_of_Alaska.svg.png

| 3. Arizona | Arizona State Nickname: The Grand Canyon State | Public Domain image on https://en.wikipedia.org/ wiki/File:2008_AZ_Proof. png |
| 4. Arkansas | The Flag of Arkansas | Public Domain Image on Wikipedia https://statesymbolsusa. org/symbol-official-item/ arkansas/state-flag/flag-ar- kansas |

| 5. California | The Great Seal of the State of California |
Photo by **James Cridland**
https://flic.kr/p/7kxcQC |
| 6. Colorado | The Flag of the State of Colorado | Public Domain Image on
https://commons.wikime-dia.org/wiki/File:Flag_of_Colorado_designed_by_Andrew_Carlisle_Carson.svg |
| 7. Connecticut | The Coat of Arms of Connecticut |
Public Domain Image on https://statesymbolsusa.org/symbol-official-item/connecticut/state-flag/flag-connecticut |

8. Delaware	Delaware State Name Origin	Public Domain Image on Wikipedia https://statesymbolsusa. org/symbol-official-item/ delaware/state-name-ori- gin/origin-delaware
9. Florida	Florida State Beverage: Orange Juice	Public Domain Photo by Scott Bauer https://statesymbolsusa. org/symbol-official-item/ florida/state-food-agricul- ture-symbol/orange-juice

10. Georgia	Georgia State Crop: Peanut	Photo by **Daniella Segura** https://flic.kr/p/dVBXdt https://statesymbolsusa. org/symbol-official-item/ georgia/state-food-agri- culture-symbol/peanut
11. Hawaii	The Flag of the State of Hawaii	Photo by **Scazon** https://flic.kr/p/5DyGJv
12. Idaho	Idaho State Fossil: Hagerman Horse Fossil	Public Domain Image on Wikipedia https://commons.wikime- dia.org/wiki/File:Equus_ simplicidens_UMNH. jpg#/media/File:Equus_ simplicidens_UMNH.jpg

| 13. Illinois | Seal of Illinois (1867) | Public Domain Image On https://statesymbolsusa. org/symbol-official-item/ illinois/state-seal/seal-il- linois |
| 14. Indiana | The Flag of Indiana | Public Domain photo on https://statesymbolsusa. org/symbol-official-item/ indiana/state-flag/flag-in- diana |

15. Iowa	Iowa State Flag	Public Domain Image on https://en.wikipedia.org/ wiki/File:Flag_of_Iowa. svg
16. Kansas	Kansas State Seal	Public Domain Image on https://en.wikipedia.org/ wiki/File:Seal_of_Kansas. svg

17. Kentucky	Kentucky Center for African American Heritage	Photo by **J.H Fenton**/ Wikipedia https://statesymbolsusa. org/symbol-official-item/ kentucky/cultural-eth- nic-org-state-cultural-her- itage/kentucky-center-af- rican
18. Louisiana	Seal of Louisiana (1902)	Public Image on https://commons.wikime- dia.org/wiki/File:Seal_of_ Louisiana.svg

| 19. Maine | State Animal: Moose | Photo by **Gail Fisher** |
| 20. Maryland | Maryland State Name Origin | Photo by **Lisby**/Flickr https://statesymbolsusa. org/symbol-official-item/ maryland/state-name-ori- gin/origin-maryland |

21. Massachusetts	Coat of Arms	Public Domain Image on https://en.wikipedia.org/ wiki/File:Flag_of_Massa- chusetts.svg
22. Michigan	Michigan State Nickname: Great Lakes State	Public Domain Image on https://en.wikipedia.org/ wiki/File:2004_MI_Proof. png

23. Minnesota	Minnesota State Nickname: The North Star State	Public Domain Image on https://statesymbolsusa. org/symbol-official-item/ minnesota/state-nick-name-state-quarter/north-star-state
24. Mississippi	Mississippi State Water Mammal: Bottlenose Dolphin	Photo by **Steven Straiton** on Flickr https://flic.kr/p/oTSCsz

25. Missouri	Missouri State Flag	Public Domain Image on Wikipedia https://en.wikipedia.org/ wiki/Missouri#media-viewer/File:Flag_of_Mis-souri.svg
26. Montana	The Flag of Montana	Public Domain Image https://commons.wikime-dia.org/wiki/File:Flag_of_Montana.svg

27. Nebraska	Nebraska State Fossil: Mammoth	Photo by Rob **Pongsaja-pan** on Flickr https://flic.kr/p/geMQJ
28. Nevada	Nevada State Flag	Photo by **Open Clip Art Library** https://commons.wikime-dia.org/wiki/File:Flag_of Nevada.svg

29. New Hampshire	Live Free or Die	Public Domain Image https://statesymbolsusa. org/sites/statesymbolsusa. org/files/primary-images/ NewHampshire-quar- terNH.jpg
30. New Jersey	Seal of New Jersey 1777 (modified in 1928).	Public Domain Image on https://commons.wikime- dia.org/wiki/File:Seal_of_ New_Jersey.svg

31. New Mexico	State flower: Yucca Flowers	Photo by **DM** on Flickr https://statesymbolsusa. org/sites/statesymbolsu- sa.org/files/styles/large/ public/primary-images/ YuccaFlowersclose.jpg?i- tok=L5XECRcD
32. New York	Seal of New York (1778)	Public Domain Image on https://commons.wikime- dia.org/wiki/File:Seal_of_ New_York.svg

33. North Carolina	North Carolina State Mineral: Gold	Photo by **Eden, Janine and Jim** on Flickr https://flic.kr/p/fTgdyT
34. North Dakota	State Fish: Northern Pike	Photo illustration by **Tom Kelly** https://statesymbolsusa. org/symbol-official-item/ north-dakota/state-fish- aquatic-life/northern-pike
35. Ohio	State tree: Ohio Buckeye	Photo by **Ruth Hartnup** https://flic.kr/p/pGbya8

36. Oklahoma	Oklahoma State Capital: Oklahoma City	Photo by **Serge Melki** on Flickr https://flic.kr/p/4QSjVr
37. Oregon	Oregon State Tree: Douglas Fir	Photo by **Tom Brandt** on Flickr https://flic.kr/p/9xqvpU
38. Pennsylvania	Aircraft: Piper J-3 Cub	Photo by **Jerry Gunner** https://statesymbolsusa. org/symbol-official-item/ pennsylvania/vessels-air- craft/piper-j-3-cub

39. Rhode Island	Rhode Island State Marine Mammal: Harbor Seal	Photo by **Tony Hisgett** on Flickr https://flic.kr/p/pJgbcY
40. South Carolina	State Flag	Public Domain Image on https://commons.wikime-dia.org/wiki/File:Flag_of_South_Carolina.svg
41. South Dakota	Flag of the State of South Dakota	Image on https://statesymbolsusa.org/symbol-official-item/south-dakota/state-flag/flag-south-dakota

42. Tennessee	Tennessee State Animal: Raccoon	Photo by **Neil McIntosh** on Flickr
		https://flic.kr/p/KsenK
43. Texas	Texas State Bread: Pan de Campo	Photo by **Steve Ryan** on Flickr
		https://statesymbolsusa. org/symbol-official-item/ texas/state-food-agricul- ture-symbol/pan-de-cam- po

44. Utah	Rocky Mountain Elk (1971)	Photo by **Andrew E. Russell** https://flic.kr/p/p4nAZN
45. Vermont	Vermont State Animal: Morgan Horse	Photo by **Anthony Domire Jr.** https://en.wikipedia.org/ wiki/File:ChestnutSilver. jpg
46. Virginia	Virginia State Dog: American Foxhound	Wikimedia Commons https://en.wikipedia.org/ wiki/File:AmericanFox- hound2.jpg

47. Washington	Washington State Seal	Image on Wikipedia
		https://statesymbolsusa. org/symbol/washington/ state-seal/seal-washington
48. West Virginia	State Flower: Rhododendron	Photo by **Arx Fortis** https://en.wikipedia.org/ wiki/File:Rhododendron maximum.jpg

| 49. Wisconsin | State Fish: Muskellunge | Public Domain USFWS Image on https://statesymbolsusa.org/symbol/wisconsin/state-fish/muskellunge |
| 50. Wyoming | Wyoming State Bird: Western Meadowlark | Photo by **Paul Hurtado** https://flic.kr/p/nW7Sba |

MOTTOS OF THE 50 U.S. STATES

These are phrases or sayings chosen by a nation, an institution, or a group of people or individuals which contain the beliefs or ideals that guide them. Mottos often invoke a sense of patriotism in people and inspire a sense of pride in their nation. The official motto of the U.S.A is "In God We Trust".

1. Alabama

- Motto
- We Dare Defend Our Rights

2. Alaska

- Motto
- North to The Future

3. Arizona

- Motto
- God Enriches

4. Arkansas

- Motto
- The People Rule

5. California

- Motto
- I Have Found It

6. Colorado

- Motto
- Nothing Without the Deity

7. Connecticut

- Motto
- He Who Transplanted Sustains

8. Delaware

- Motto
- Liberty and Independence

9
Florida

Motto

In God We Trust

10. Georgia

Motto

Wisdom, Justice, and Moderation

11. Hawaii

Motto

The Life of the Land is Perpetuated in Righteousness

12. Idaho

Motto

Let It Be Perpetual

13. Illinois

- Motto
- State Sovereignty, National Union

14. Indiana

- Motto
- The Crossroads Of America

15. Iowa

- Motto
- Our Liberties We Prize and Our Rights We Will Maintain

16. Kansas

- Motto
- To the Stars Through Difficulties

17. Kentucky

- Motto
- United We Stand, Divided We Fall

18. Louisiana

- Motto
- Union, Justice, Confidence

19. Maine

- Motto
- I Lead

20. Maryland

- Motto
- Manly Deeds, Womanly Words

21. Massachusetts

- Motto
- By the Sword We Seek Peace, But Peace Only Under Liberty

22. Michigan

- Motto
- If You Seek a Pleasant Peninsula, Look About You

23. Minnesota

- Motto
- The Star of the North

24. Mississippi

- Motto
- By Valor and Arms

25. Missouri

- Motto
- Let the Welfare of the People Be the Supreme Law

26. Montana

- Motto
- God and Silver

27. Nebraska

- Motto
- Equality Before the Law

28. Nevada

- Motto
- All for Our Country And Battle Born

29. New Hampshire

- Motto
- Live Free or Die

30. New Jersey

- Motto
- Liberty And Prosperity

31. New Mexico

- Motto
- It Grows as It Goes

32. New York

- Motto
- Excelsior— Ever Upward

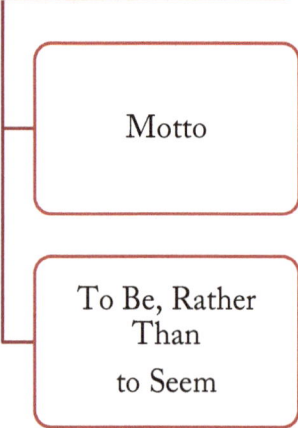

33.
North Carolina

Motto

To Be, Rather Than
to Seem

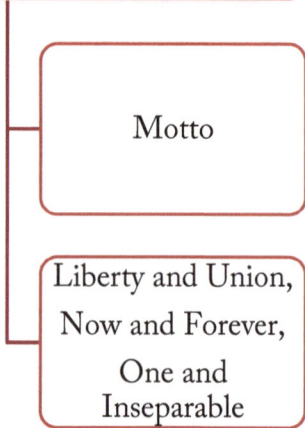

34.
North Dakota

Motto

Liberty and Union,
Now and Forever,
One and
Inseparable

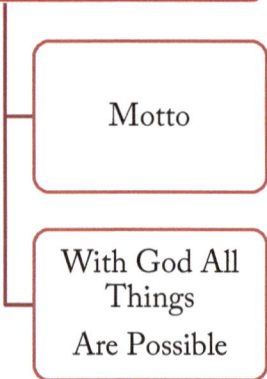

35.
Ohio

Motto

With God All
Things
Are Possible

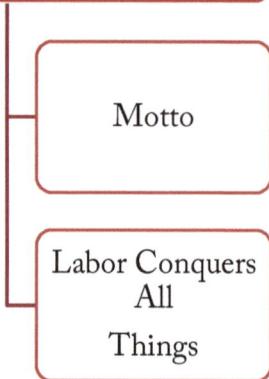

36.
Oklahoma

Motto

Labor Conquers
All
Things

37.
Oregon

- Motto

- She Flies with Her
  Own Wings

38.
Pennsylvania

- Motto

- Virtue, Liberty, and
  Independence

39.
Rhode Island

- Motto

- Hope

40.
South Carolina

- Motto

- While I Breath, I Hope Ready in Soul
  and Resource

41. South Dakota

- Motto
- Under God, The People Rule

42. Tennessee

- Motto
- Agriculture and Commerce

43. Texas

- Motto
- Friendship

44. Utah

- Motto
- Industry

45. Vermont

- Motto
- Freedom and Unity

46. Virginia

- Motto
- Thus Always to Tyrants

47. Washington

- Motto
- By and By

48. West Virginia

- Motto
- Mountaineers Are Always Free

49. Wisconsin

- Motto
- Forward

50. Wyoming

- Motto
- Equal Rights

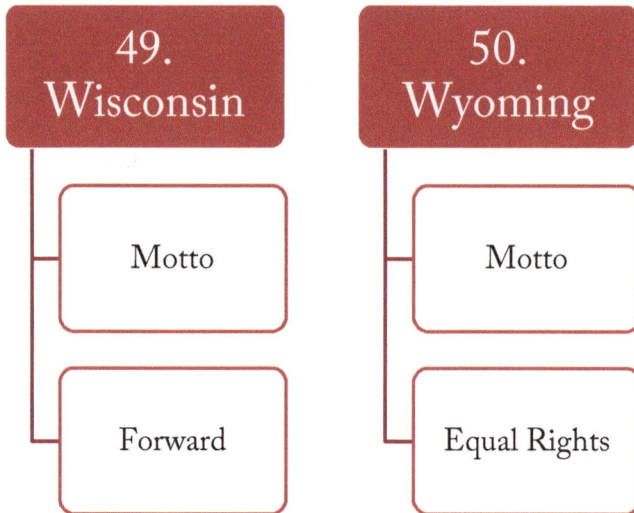

Source: https://state.1keydata.com/state-mottos.php

MYTHS AND LEGENDS OF AMERICA

America has a long list of myths and legends especially about the indigenous people—referred to as Native Americans or American Indians—and the tribes that occupied this land centuries ago. I will mention a few that caught my roving eye and cracked my ribs!

The **Pima Indians of Arizona** recount that the father of all men and animals was the butterfly called **Cherwit Make**, or Earth Maker. It is said Cherwit fluttered down from the clouds to the blue cliffs at the junction of the Verde and Salt Rivers, and from his own sweat, men were created. The legend goes on to say that as people grew in numbers they became selfish and quarrelsome and this did not please Cherwit. He vowed to destroy them all by drowning them, but before that could happen he told them to be honest and live at peace with one another.

The people did not listen to him, nor did they listen to the messenger he sent called Suha. The evil in the world continued, but before Suha passed on, he foretold that people would become arrogant with wealth, envious of the property of others, and would wage wars for profit. "When this comes to pass", Suha said. "Another flood will come and wipe out the bad people whereas the good ones will go and live in the sun."

Source: https://www.legendsofamerica.com/ah-arksuperstition mountains/

Did you know that **Death Valley in California** was named by a group of California-bound white pioneers, prospecting for gold? These pioneers first came to the valley after splitting off from a wagon train headed out of Utah in 1849, and later were lost in the valley themselves. It is said these emigrants became known as the Forty Niners, and when they later found their way out of the valley, they declared, "Goodbye, Death Valley."

Source: https://www.legendsofamerica.com/ca-deathvalley/
https://www.legendsofamerica.com/ca-lost49ers/

Death Valley Caves by Charles M. Skinner

These Forty Niners remind me of the professional American Football Team, the 49ers who play at Levi's Stadium in Santa Clara, California. Located in the San Francisco Bay Area and founded in 1946, this football team ranks third today in the National Football League (NFL) and was named after the gold prospectors mentioned above who arrived in Northern California in 1849 during the Gold Rush.

The following section about Death Valley is no myth, so take note:

Death Valley is one of the hottest, driest, and lowest places on Earth. In summer, temperatures average over 116 degrees Fahrenheit. Death Valley is considered by scientists the hottest place on Earth.

In 1913, a temperature of 56.70 Centigrade(C) or 134.060 Fahrenheit(F) was recorded in Death Valley. It is the driest place in the USA. The Mojave Desert locale (a favorite hiking area) in the valley, experienced the hottest temperatures on record in June 2016, as stated by the article "The 14 Hottest Places on Earth" by **Logan Orlando** and **Caitlin Morton** on cntraveler.com (June 15,2017). The second hottest place on earth is **Aziziyah** in Libya on the African Continent. It is 25 miles south of Tripoli, the capital of Libya. Aziziyah regularly experiences temperatures of over 480C or 118.40F in mid-summer.

The third hottest place on earth is **Dallol**, in Ethiopia. This geological wonderland of salt formations, acidic hot springs, and gas geysers, records average summer temperatures of up to 114°Fahrenheit(F).

Source: https://www.independent.co.uk/travel/news-and-advice/ weather-heatwave-latest-hottest-places-on-earth-death-valley-aziziyah-dallol-wadi-halfa-lut-desert-a7802366.html , https://www. cntraveler.com/galleries/2015-11-27/the-hottest-places-in-the-world , https://www.livescience.com/19700-hottest-place-earth.html

Riders of the Desert or Ghost Riders is the tale of a Native American by the name of Ta-in-ga-ro, or First Falling Thunder, who tied a Spanish trader on a horse with the corpse of his own wife, face-to-face, and left the Spanish for dead in the desert. This was after the Native American discovered that the Spaniard had tricked him into leaving his wife Zecana, or The Bird, under the Spanish man's custody while First Falling Thunder was away in the heart of the mountains. The intention of the Spanish trader was to take the beautiful Zacana from Ta-in-ga-ro.

On his return from the expedition—which turned sour after he saw a distressed Zecana in a pool of water, resulting from having cast beads and wampum into the spring waters in Manitou thus angering the deity of the well—Ta-in-ga-ro discovered that Zecana had lost her mind due to the treachery of the Spanish trader.

The self-inflicted death of Zecana after plucking a knife from her husband's belt and thrusting it into her heart, led Ta-in-ga-ro to hunt down the Spanish man. He was never far behind the Spaniard and the dead corpse of Zecana until the Spanish trader ran mad due to the torturous conditions created by Ta-in-ga-ro and the harsh desert.

It was then that Ta-in-ga-ro let go of the horse's reins and watched the horse with its dead and manic rider disappear into the desert void. The legend ends by saying that from that day onward, the ghost rider has continued to wander to and fro, through the bush, the sand, and the salt conditions of the plain. This is believed to have occurred in the sandstone columns of the Colorado Foot-Hills.

Source: https://www.legendsofamerica.com/co-riderdesert/

The Yellowstone Tragedy is the tale of a few brave Native Americans who decided to fight and later died rather than be taken prisoner on account of white settler protective soldiers who drove them from the settlements in the geyser basins and mountains of the upper Yellowstone Country in what today is the state of Montana. This event must have happened between the mid 1800's and early 1900's when there was great hostility between the early white settlers and the different Native American tribes. It was not uncommon for these Native Americans to attack travelling parties of station wagons and caravans, including the guards and soldiers who were dispatched to protect unarmed and sometimes armed civilians.

On a regular basis, Native Americans deliberately attacked soldier outposts, killed and wounded men, women, and children, and looted and destroy property. The most notorious period of this banditry throughout the great plains and valleys of present day Colorado, Kansas, Nebraska, North Dakota, Montana, Wyoming, and New Mexico, took place between 1854 and 1870. This was during the early settlements and emigration to Colorado and the discovery of gold in the Rocky Mountains.

The remnants of the fugitive band at the center of this legend were from the Crow tribe, also called Absaroka. Historically, this tribe lived in the Yellowstone River Valley. The Crow were skilled horsemen and hunters from Montana. They hunted mountain deer, sheep, other game, and Bison or American Buffalo, their main source of meat. The legend goes that these remnant Native Americans gathered at the head of the mighty rift known as the Grand Canyon of the Yellowstone and built a raft which they used to try and escape on the stream when soldiers came after them and started shooting.

The Native Americans loved the mountains and the land at the head of the river because their forefathers had used it as hunting ground for centuries. Interestingly, these Native Americans feared the geysers and the hissing noise they created in the basins. They thought the geysers had evil spirits inside them. However, they looked at the mountains at the head of the river as the top of the world. They believed that whoever reached the top would be able to see the "happy hunting grounds below, brightened with the homes of the blessed" —a line written by Charles M. Skinner in 1896. That is why they wanted to live on the other side of the mountains of the Yellowstone.

Source: https://www.legendsofamerica.com/wy-yellowstonetragedy/ ,

https://www.legendsofamerica.com/na-crow/ ,

https://www.legendsofamerica.com/we-overlandtrail/

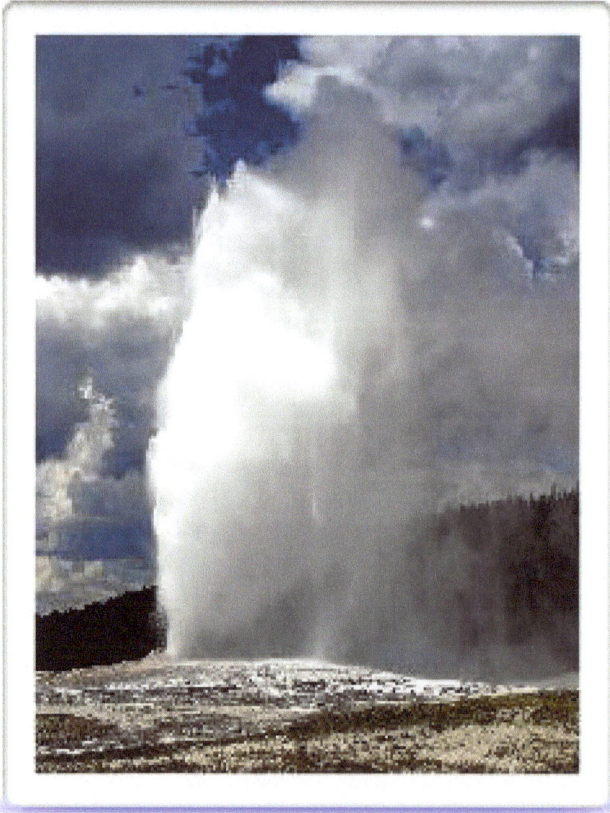

Yellowstone County Geyser "Old Faithful"
(photo by: Charles M. Skinner)

3

GOVERNMENT

The United States of America is run by the Federal Government under a federal republic.

This government is the umbrella body of the 50 States, one district—Washington, D.C., the nation's capital, and several territories.

The federal government has arms or branches that help run its activities. These are the Legislative (Congress), Executive (President), and Judiciary (Courts) branches. The United States Constitution, which is considered the supreme or highest law of the land, gives powers to the above branches to exercise their authority. The above system of government is also duplicated on a smaller scale in the 50 States of the U.S.

Each of the 50 States has their own smaller legislative, executive, and judiciary branch governed by the State constitution, and is therefore responsible for the running of the affairs of that particular state. It is important to note, however, that these 50 states share some of the responsibilities of the federal government but at a lower level.

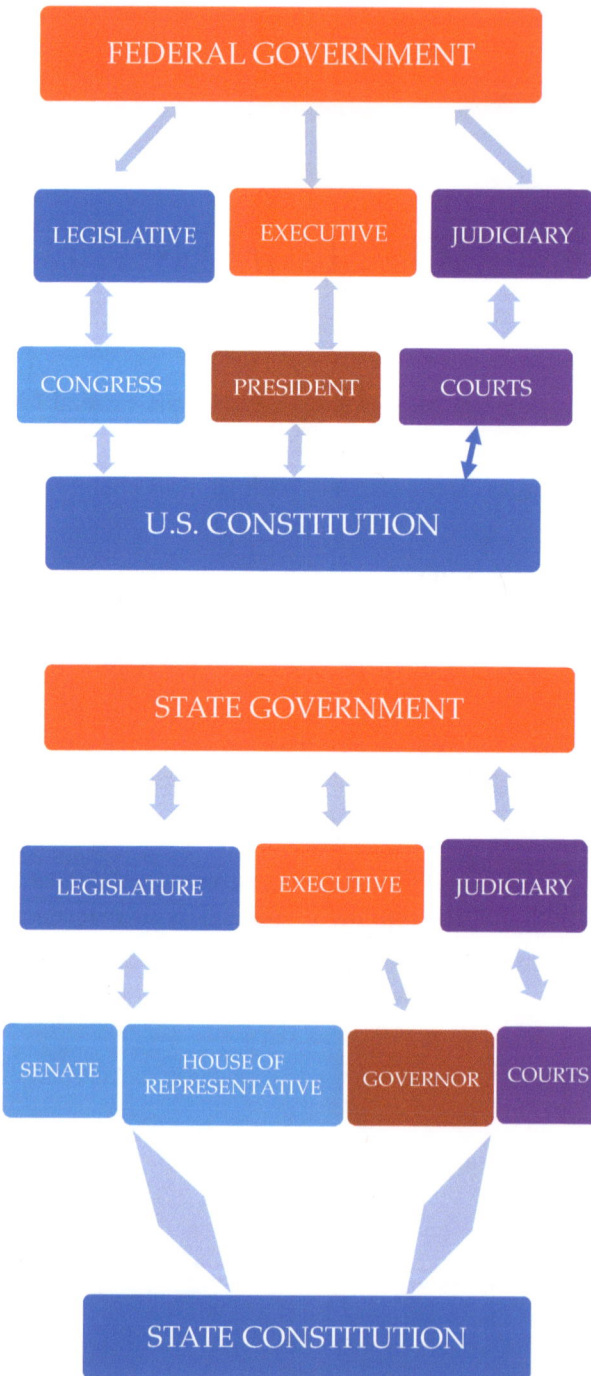

4

THE PEOPLE

The United States of America has an estimated population of 328.83 million people according to the live population clock, ranking the country third in the world in terms of population as of October 20, 2018. This is according to census.gov, the United States Census Bureau.

Most of this population live in urban areas. The U.S. is a racially and ethnically diverse population that brings together people from all walks of life with a common purpose: To live the American Dream, and for this country to be a beacon of hope to all those people who aspire to work hard and play fair in the pursuit of happiness.

There are six racial categories of people recognized by the U.S. Bureau of Census. These are White American, Black or African American, American Indian, Asian American, Alaska Native, Native Hawaiian or Pacific Islander, and two or more races simply referred to as "some other race". Hispanic or Latino Americans are considered an ethnicity not a race.

In the United States of America, White Americans make up most of the population, totaling 76.9%, while African Americans are the largest racial minority group with a population of 12.7%, according to the July 2016 data provided by wikipedia.org. Hispanic and Latino Americans account for 17.8% of the population. They also happen to be the largest ethnic minority group in America.

The diversity and ethnicity of Americans can be traced from the many places these Americans originally came from, like Great Britain, Ireland, Italy, Japan, Germany, India, Africa, Russia, China. The diversity of Americans can also be traced by reviewing who these Americans are in terms of religious beliefs and lifestyle, like Christians, Buddhists, and Moslems to mention a few.

This diversity has created a rich cultural heritage each celebrated in the cities and urban towns of America through festivals, dance, live-music, cultural galas, exhibitions, and fun-fairs.

The coming together of all these people from the different corners of the world to live and work in the U.S., has given this country the name "Land of the Immigrant", "Land of the Free", and "The Greatest Country in the World"!

While the U.S. ranks 3rd in world population with 327.47 million people as of October 20, 2018, China ranks number one with 1.41 billion people; India ranks second with 1.35 billion people; Indonesia comes fourth with 267.65 million people; and Brazil is fifth with 211.35 million people. New York City is the most populous city in America with 8.6 million people.

Vatican City or the Holy See has the smallest population of only 804 people according to the live population clock as of October 20, 2018.

N.B.: It is estimated that by 2020, the U.S. population will be 331.43 million people and 84.1% of the population will be urban. This data is based on the latest United Nations Population Division estimates of 2018 and on current estimates of the live population clock, historical data, and projected figures.

Source: http://www.worldometers.info/world-population/population-by-country/ ,

https://census.gov/en.html,

http://worldpopulationreview.com/countries/

5

QUALITY OF LIFE
IN THE U.S.

Quality of life in the United States of America varies from one state to another. This has to do with how people and the environment relate to each other. In America, the Clean Air Act, the Clean Water Act, and Safe Drinking Water Act, ensure that states properly dispose of pollutants and that public drinking water meets federal standards. This law helps preserve natural resources and protects the public from harmful toxins that would affect their quality of life.

A person's well-being is largely determined by his/her interactions with those around him/her and the feeling that they are socially supported. This experience brings greater happiness as well as physical and mental health.

In 2018, U.S. News and World Report published data telling us which states in America have the highest quality of life. The data looked at the natural environment (quality of water, quality of air, pollution, and industrial toxins) and the social environment (community engagement, like spending time with family members and friends, social support, and voter participation in 2016 elections).

Below are the best states according to quality of life ranked from one to fifty.

RANKING	STATE	ABBREVIATION OF STATE
1	NORTH DAKOTA	ND
2	MINNESOTA	MN
3	WISCONSIN	WI
4	NEW HAMP-SHIRE	NH
5	SOUTH DAKOTA	SD
6	MISSISSIPPI	MS
7	ARKANSAS	AR
8	NEW MEXICO	NM
9	IOWA	IA
10	COLORADO	CO
11	WYOMING	WY

RANKING	STATE	ABBREVIATION OF STATE
12	MAINE	ME
13	MONTANA	MT
14	NEBRASKA	NE
15	MISSOURI	MO
16	KANSAS	KS
17	OKLAHOMA	OK
18	OREGON	OR
19	ALASKA	AK
20	IDAHO	ID
21	WASHINGTON	WA

RANKING	STATE	ABBREVIATION OF STATE
22	UTAH	UT
23	RHODE ISLAND	RI
24	DELAWARE	DE
25	MASSACHU-SETTS	MA
26	VERMONT	VT
27	KENTUCKY	KY

RANKING	STATE	ABBREVIATION OF STATE
28	TENNESSEE	TN
29	MICHIGAN	MI
30	SOUTH CAROLI-NA	SC
31	MARYLAND	MD
32	GEORGIA	GA
33	FLORIDA	FL
34	NORTH CAROLINA	NC
35	ALABAMA	AL

RANKING	STATE	ABBREVIATION OF STATE
36	HAWAII	HI
37	NEW YORK	NY
38	CONNECTICUT	CT
39	ARIZONA	AZ
40	OHIO	OH
41	VIRGINIA	VA

RANKING	STATE	ABBREVIATION OF STATE
42	LOUISIANA	LA
43	NEVADA	NV
44	PENNSYLVANIA	PA
45	WEST VIRGINIA	WV
46	TEXAS	TX
47	ILLINOIS	IL
48	INDIANA	IN
49	NEW JERSEY	NJ
50	CALIFORNIA	CA

Data Source: https://www.usnews.com/news/best-states/rankings/quality-of-life

Taking a global look at the world over, quality of life in each country is determined by many things, like economic influence, power, citizenship, and social well-being. Other aspects of quality of life include economic stability, affordability or the ability to buy goods and services at a cheap price, quality of local job market, income equality, and family friendliness. Political stability, safety, quality of public health, and quality of public education are determinants too of any country's well-being.

Below are 10 countries said to offer the best quality of life. In other words, these are the best countries to live in, according to the 2018 U.S. News and World Report.

RANKING	COUNTRY	IMAGE
1	CANADA	photo by **Scott Webb**

2	DENMARK	 Source: https://pixabay.com/photo-3105058/
3	SWEDEN	photo by **Frans Van Heerden**
4	NORWAY	Source: https://pixabay.com/en/sheep-mountains-norway-landscape-3744175/

5	AUSTRALIA	photo by **Patrick Mc Lachlan**
6	SWITZERLAND	Source: https://pixabay.com/en/ lake-lucerne-region-foun- tain-3723559/
7	FINLAND	Finnish, Oak Island Source: https://pixabay.com/en/finn- ish-oak-island-restaurant-kni- pan-3454898/

8	NETHERLANDS	source: https://cdn. pixabay.com/pho-to/2016/06/26/21/38/tram-1481395_1280.jpg
9	NEW ZEALAND	photo by **Ketan Kumawat**
10	GERMANY	photo by **Ingo Joseph**

N.B.: The United States of America ranks number 17 in countries with the best quality of life. However, the U.S. ranks number 8 in the overall best countries to live in. The overall best countries have a lot to do with the strength of their GDP rather than other attributes. Therefore, being wealthy does not necessarily mean that country is the best place to live. Gross Domestic Product or GDP is the sum of the market values, or prices, of all final goods and services produced in an economy during a period of time, often annually or quarterly.

The best countries ranking was derived from nine sub-rankings of the 65 country attributes—terms that can be used to describe a country and are relevant to the success of a modern nation. Each country was scored on each of the 65 country attributes based on a collection of individual survey responses.

According to the survey released at the beginning of 2018 by usnews.com, "The more a country was perceived to exemplify a certain characteristic in relation to the average, the higher that country's attribute score and vice versa."

To come up with the best overall countries score, the weight of each sub-ranking was correlated to the 2014 gross domestic product purchasing power parity per capita, a measure of inclusive prosperity, as reported by the International Monetary Fund (IMF).

Source: https://www.usnews.com/news/best-countries/articles/methodology , https://www.cnbc.com/2018/01/27/us-news-world-report-10-countries-with-the-best-quality-of-life.html ,

https://www.usnews.com/news/best-countries/overall-full-list#

LIFE EXPECTANCY

Life expectancy in the U.S. has continued to fall for the second year in a row. This is according to a 2017/2018 Annual Report by the Centers for Disease Control and Prevention (CDC).

The life expectancy of an American baby born today is estimated to live on average 78.6 years, down from 78.9 years in 2014.

The leading causes of death in America are **heart disease** and **cancer**. Drug overdoses has now climbed to third place from fourth in 2015. Other statistics according to the annual report suggest that the epidemic of **addiction to opioids** is causing this alarming trend. The continued fall in life expectancy in the United States of America is due to the above fatal illnesses of cancer, heart disease, drug overdoses and use, and suicide deaths among other illnesses.

Source: https://www.economist.com/united-states/2018/01/04/life-expectancy-in-america-has-declined-for-two-years-in-a-row , https://www.cdc.gov/nchs/data/hus/hus17.pdf#highlights

The world over, **Japan** has the highest life expectancy at 84.2 years followed by Switzerland 83.3 years and Spain 83.1 years. This is according to the World Health Organization data of the life expectancy of countries in 2016. Singapore comes fourth at 82.9 years. The fourth spot is also shared with Australia and France at 82.9 years respectively. Canada follows with 82.8 years and Italy with 82.8 years likewise. The Republic of Korea comes next with a life expectancy of 82.7 years. Norway has 82.5 years, followed by Sweden and Iceland with 82.4 years.

The country with the lowest life expectancy is Lesotho at 52.9 years, followed by the Central African Republic at 53 years and Sierra Leone at 53.1 years.

The data explaining the gap in life expectancy between one country and another and between the country with the highest and lowest life expectancy is not provided, but it is my understanding that this variation depends on how much or how less these countries are affected by the factors leading to a reduction in the life expectancy.

Source: http://apps.who.int/gho/data/node.main.688?lang=en ,

6

AMERICAN CULTURE

Statue of Liberty

The way people live and work in America has been influenced by different cultures, traditions, and customs. This influence is internal and external and has varied from the effect of immigrant communities in the United States to various customs and traditions from other countries.

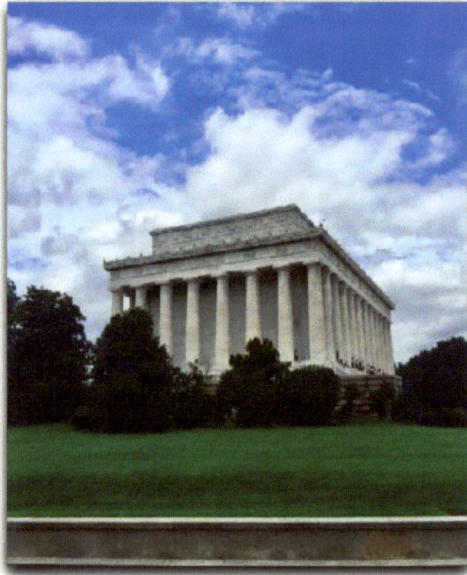

Lincoln Memorial (Washington D.C.)

Population in the U.S. was and is still built on immigration from other countries. America is sometimes called "A Melting Pot" due to this mix of different cultures. American culture like any other includes religion, food, language, music, dress, style, moral beliefs (right and wrong), marriage (the history, purpose, and changing trends), and hospitality—not forgetting the entertainment industry and the country's architecture.

According to the U.S. Census Bureau, a child is born every 8 seconds and a person dies every 12 seconds. A new immigrant comes to the U.S. every 33 seconds. It is also said that the United States has the most diverse culture in the entire world. This diversity includes the English who came to the "New Colony" in the 1600's, the Native Americans found already residing on the main land, Asians, Africans Arabs from the Middle-East, Turks, Jews, Persians, and Latin Americans.

With this mix of cultures and peoples, you would expect the American people to speak several languages. Indeed, according to the U.S.

Census Bureau and American Community Survey (ACS) 2016 Language Data Overhaul, there are 1,333 **languages** spoken in the U.S. This contrasts drastically from the 384 languages spoken in the U.S. in 2015. The reason for this change is that many languages that were previously on the code list needed to receive updated definitions or labels that were more transparent to the users. Many languages were grouped into one code. For example, in 2015, all speakers of French-based Creole were coded as "French Creole" and many people wanted to know the composition of languages in that group. The new coding of specific languages going forward is in accordance with the International Organization for Standardization's ISO-639-3 standard. It will also enable the Census Bureau present languages in terms understood by linguists and translators.

The survey and Census Bureau state that the updated data tables will not provide separate estimates for all 1,333 languages, but will group together recognizable languages large enough for people to provide reliable estimates. This new information is contained in the article "Inside the American Community Survey: 2016 Language Data Overhaul", written on September 14th 2017 by **Christine Gambino** from the Social, Economic, and Housing Statistics Division of the Census Bureau.

The United States of America has no official language on the federal level, although 90% of its population speak or understand some form of American English. Although efforts have been made at almost every session in Congress to bring an amendment in favor of adopting English as the official language, this has not translated into reality up until now. However, most official business, be it at the federal or state level, is conducted in English.

Interestingly, unlike the federal government which has no official language, 32 state governments out of 50 have declared English to be either one of, or the only official language.

Source: https://www.census.gov/newsroom/blogs/random-samplings/2017/09/inside_the_american.html ,

https://www.usconstitution.net/consttop_lang.html ,
https://en.wikipedia.org/wiki/Languages_of_the_United_States

Diversity in Unity

Different regions of the country have different immigrants who migrated there and as a result formed clusters of populations who speak a particular language apart from English.

Due to the numerous languages spoken in the United States, this book will detail some information about a few main languages spoken in America apart from the English language.

Spanish has been spoken in the U.S. since the 16th and 17th centuries with the arrival of Spanish Colonization in North America. The colonizers settled in areas which became today California, Nevada, Arizona, Utah, New Mexico, Texas, Colorado, and Florida. Today, some 45 million Hispanic and Latino Americans speak the language whose legacy and culture has spread throughout the North American Continent.

California was home to most of the **Chinese** speaking Taishanese and Cantonese until the 20th century. Mandarin, the official language in the People's Republic of China (PRC) and the Republic of China (Taiwan), has now become the prevalent language spoken since the opening of the PRC. In New York City, only 10 percent of Chinese speakers spoke Mandarin in 2002, but today, Mandarin is predicted to replace Cantonese. According to the U.S. Census Bureau's American Community Survey of 2016, 2.8 million Americans speak some variety of Chinese.

French which is the fourth-most-common language in the U.S. developed in the United States during colonial times. The three varieties that developed included Missouri French, Louisiana French, and New England French. The language is spoken mainly by the Louisiana Creole, native French, Cajun Haitian, and French-Canadian populations. The language is widely spoken in Vermont, New Hampshire, Louisiana, Maine, the northern San Francisco Bay area, and in the francophone enclaves of St. Clair County, Michigan.

With 2 million people speaking French in the United States, the largest French-speaking communities are found in Northeast Maine, Hollywood (California), Miami, Florida, and New York City.

German was widely spoken in several of the colonies, especially Pennsylvania, where German speaking Protestants and other religious minorities settled to escape persecution in Europe. Another settlement occurred in the U.S. when Germans fled the failure of the 19th century revolution. Many German immigrants settled in urban areas in many cities, speaking German and publishing newspapers and periodicals in that language. German farmers also took up farming around the country, including in Texas Hill Country. German was widely spoken in the U.S. until the United States entered World War I. One reason for the decline of the German language was the perception during the two World Wars that speaking the language of the enemy was unpatriotic.

Today, 49 million Americans claim German ancestry, the largest self-described ethnic group in the United States. While 1.2 million Americans speak German, many of whom are Amish, Mennonite, or new German immigrants, the U.S. Census Bureau's American Community Survey 2016 points out that less than 4 percent of these German-speakers use a language other than English at home.

African American culture took hold in the south and mid-west of the country due to the forced Atlantic slave trade and following liberation in the American Civil War. **African American English** often called AAE and known in North America as Black English, is a variety of American English spoken primarily by urban working-class and middle-class African Americans. Linguists and many African Americans believe Southern American English is closely related to AAE because AAE is part of a historical ongoing, and slow changing language between creoles such as Gullah and Southern American English.

Gullah is another English-African creole language that is spoken on the Sea Islands of South Carolina and Georgia. It retains strong influences of the West African languages.

Italian and its various dialects have been widely spoken in the U.S. for more than 100 years, from the late 19th century to the mid-20th century. This was due to large scale immigration during the above time period. As of 2009, the U.S. Census Bureau stated that of the 15.638 million Americans who reported being Italian-American, only 753,992 reported speaking the language on the main land.

Many Muslim Americans and immigrants from the Middle East speak several varieties of **Arabic**. The highest populations of native Arabic speakers live in the urban areas of Chicago, New York City, and Los Angeles. The U.S. Census Bureau's American Community Survey 2016 data shows that Detroit and the surrounding areas of Michigan have significant numbers of Arabic-speaking people, including many Arab Christians of Lebanese, Syrian, and Palestinian descent.

Native American languages predate European settlement in the New World, also known as the Americas. These languages continue to be spoken fluently in few parts of the U.S., like Indian reservations. Although most of these languages are endangered, there are still many small communities of Native Americans in the Southwest (Arizona and New Mexico) who make use of them.

The largest Native American speaking community is the Navajo who speak **Athabaskan**, a language of the Na-Dene´ family. They live in Utah, New Mexico, and Arizona. The Navajo make up 50 percent of all Native American language speakers in the United States.

Other Native American languages include **Western Apache** spoken mostly in Arizona; **Dakota**, a Siouan language spoken in North Dakota and South Dakota; Central Alaskan **Yup'ik**, an Eskimo-Aleut language spoken mostly in Alaska; **Cherokee**, belonging to the Iroquoian family in Oklahoma and North Carolina; and the **Oódham** language spoken by the Pima and Tohono Oódham who live in central and southern Arizona and northern Sonora. These are a few among the many Native American languages prevalent today.

The **Japanese** language is spoken mostly in the state of Hawaii, followed by the states of California, Washington, Oregon, Nevada, Alaska, New York, and Utah. There about 460,000 Americans who speak the language today.

Source : https://en.wikipedia.org/wiki/Languages_of_the_United_States , https://statisticalatlas.com/United-States/Languages

When it comes to **religion**, this western nation was founded on the basis of religious freedom. America is not an atheist country. The most current data from Wikipedia, the free encyclopedia released in October, 2018, based on data from the 2016 Gallup, Inc. shows that America is made up of 73.7% Christians (including among others Evangelical Protestant, Mainline Protestant, Catholic, Mormon, and Jehovah's Witness), 5.4% Non-Christian faiths like Islam, Judaism, and Buddhism; 18.2% of people who are unaffiliated to any religion (Atheists and Agnostics), and 2.7% of the population who did not respond to the survey.

Judaism is the second-largest religion in America, practiced by 2.1% of the population. This is followed by Islam with 0.8%. Protestants are the largest group among Christians making up 48.9% of the Christian population. Mississippi is the most religious state in the country with

63% of its population identifying itself as very religious. New Hampshire is the least religious state with only 20% of its adult population describing themselves as very religious. The most religious region of the U.S. is America Samoa, an unincorporated territory of the United States located in the South Pacific Ocean, with 99.3% of its population being religious.

Source: https://en.wikipedia.org/wiki/Religion_in_the_United_States ,

The **food or cuisine** of America was influenced by Europeans and Native Americans during the early history of the country. Today, however, we can safely say that every region of the world has had an influence on the American cuisine and culture. There are a number of styles of cooking and types of food that are specific to each region today.

For example, Southern-style cooking is often called "American comfort food" or "soul food". This is because of the great care that is taken in making each dish.

Southern style food has had heavy connections with the African slave trade culture, which marked a dark period in the history of the United States. These dishes included intestines cooked into chitlins, fat back and salted pork which replaced lean bacon, cabbage and collard greens, which then were known as weeds. While these influences have been passed on to the present generation in the deep south, other dishes present include fried chicken, black-eyed peas, and corn bread. The reasons African slaves resorted to this food was because they did not have access to the prime cuts of meat, quality ingredients, and often working kitchens, according to the recipes website.

Tex-Mex is Mexican cuisine with roots in Spanish cooking, whipped up in the Texas style. These dishes include steak fajitas, nachos, and chimichangas. The roots of the burrito is believed to be in Los Angeles, but soon spread southeast to Texas. Beef and cheese are Texas additions to this Mexican cuisine.

The Creole cuisine, famous in Louisiana, has roots in French ingredients and techniques, combined with Spanish, African, and Caribbean influences. Oyster Rockfeller is one of the foods from this group. Green peppers, onion, and celery are the hallmarks of the culinary Creole "Holy Trinity", another example of French influences according to the website recipes.howstuffworks.com.

In Hawaii, the food is influenced by Japanese, Filipino, Korean, Chinese, Portuguese, and Polynesian cuisine. These influences are due to the immigration of people from the above nationalities who worked on the Pineapple and Sugar Cane plantations. For example, the Chinese brought fried rice, sweet and sour, and dim sum; Japanese sushi also had a lot of influence; Spain brought spice; the Portuguese introduced salted fish dishes; open-fire Korean barbecue dishes came along; and the introduction of fried food, peas, and beans came from the Philippines.

Seafood, meat pies, cheese, cream, and butter-based dishes, are the staple foods of the Northeastern region of the United States. New England owes much of its culinary culture to the influences of the first settlers and in part to the rich availability of food in the ocean of the region. The puritan settlers were more accustomed to baking than frying food, thus the meat pies cited above. There was also an influence of Native Americans in the food chain history, that's why foods like the corn-based Jonny-cakes and hasty pudding exist.

On the whole, however, America is known for hamburgers, potato chips, french-fries, hot dogs, macaroni and cheese, apple pie, and meat loaf.

Source: https://www.livescience.com/28945-american-culture.html , https://recipes.howstuffworks.com/menus/5-influences-on-regional-cooking.htm

Music wise, the U.S. has different styles of music which include folk, popular, and classical music. The different genres of the styles above include traditional folk music and roots that encompasses bluegrass, gospel, Appalachian folk, blues, Cajun, and Native American music.

Popular genres include rock, country, gospel, soul, disco, ragtime, jazz, R&B, house, techno, hip hop, salsa, and grunge; then classical music which influenced American folk music styles in the 18th century, and by folk, jazz, blues, Native American, and pop styles from the 20th century until today.

The influences on music in the United States have come from France, Spain, Scotland, England, West Africa, Ireland, Wales, Japan, Poland, India, German, Russia, Italy, and Latin America—just to mention a few.

Today, the most popular music in America includes hip hop, rock, country, soul, jazz, rhythm and blues (R&B), heavy metal, punk (a rock music genre developed in the mid 1970's in the United States, United Kingdom, and Australia), and funk (a rhythmic and danceable music from a mixture of jazz, soul music, and R&B) that originated in African American communities in the mid 1960's.

Source: https://en.wikipedia.org/wiki/Music_history_of_the_United _States

Night Life at a Discotheque

The **fashion** industry and style in America has been and continues to be heavily influenced by celebrities and the media. Celebrities and the media are heavily influenced by fashion designers, whether based in the United States or elsewhere, who have transformed the way women and men think about clothing and style.

The most notable place to observe fashion's most effective designs and the celebrities who wear these designs is the red carpet in Hollywood. Functions like the Oscars (Academy Awards of the film industry) and the Emmy Awards (an American Award recognizing excellence in the television industry), fashion designers showcase their products and designs which in turn have a strong influence on the designs and fashion of clothing the public wears.

Notable designers that have made their mark on the American fashion industry include but are not limited to **Coco Chanel**, a French fashion designer and founder of the well-known Chanel brand; **Donna Karen**, the sole creator of DKNY label (Donna Karen New York); **Giorgio Armani**, founder of the fashion power house Armani; **Calvin Klein**, a New Yorker who has dominated the fashion world for over 75 years; and **Donatella Versace**, a power house of fabulous collections of clothing, accessories, fragrances, and home furnishings.

Others include **Ralph Lauren**, a designer of women's suits designed in the classic men's style, and the designer of the short-sleeved shirts with the renowned polo emblem on them; **Christian Dior** , was a French fashion designer best known as the founder of one of the world's top fashion houses, also called Christian Dior. Now owned by Groupe Arnault, Christian Dior fashion houses are all-over the world. The brand specializes in designing women's costume gowns, swirling full skirts and nipped-in waists with fitted jackets, feminine silhouettes, suits, dresses, and accessories like perfumes; **Tom Ford**, a Texan born designer who has become extremely famous, creating high-end fashion and accessories; and **Pierre Cardin** and **Yves Saint Laurent** who redesigned traditionally masculine clothing into beautiful, feminine pieces for women.

Source: https://www.lovehappensmag.com/blog/top-50-fashion-designers/

America is known for jeans, cowboy hats, boots, sneakers, and base-ball caps.

Popular brands of well-known clothing include Calvin Klein, Victoria Secret, Michael Kors, Nike, Old Navy, Ralph Lauren, and Levi Strauss & Company.

We are moving very fast so let's take a breather:

It's
quiz
time

Question: Can you name the ten most successful songs that have featured on America's Billboard since its inception in 1958? Or the five hottest male and female American singers? I bet you might have some idea about these, but right now, here are the answers.

The 10 All Time Greatest Songs on the American Billboard

Answers to quiz question.

1. Chubby Checker—"The Twist", 1960
2. Santana—"Smooth", featuring Rob Thomas, 1999
3. Bobby Darin—"Mack The Knife", 1959
4. LeAnn Rimes—"How Do I Live", 1997
5. LMFAO—"Party Rock Anthem", featuring Lauren Bennet & Goon Rock, 2011
6. The Black Eyed Peas—"I Gotta Feeling", 2009
7. Los Del Rio—"Macarena (Bayside Boys Mix), 1996
8. Olivia Newton-John—"Physical", 1981
9. Debbie Boone—"You Light Up My Life", 1997
10. The Beatles—"Hey Jude", 1968

Source:https://www.billboard.com/articles/events/greatest-of-all-time/6760872/billboard-greatest-of-all-time-charts-top-songs-album-acts

The Handsomest/Hottest American Male Singer

1. Adam Noah Levine—Maroon5, pop music, contemporary R&B, rock music, etc.
2. Kurt Cobain—alternative rock, punk rock, grunge.
3. Justine Timberlake—hip hop music, pop music, electronica, etc.
4. Jared Leto—thirty seconds to Mars Band.
5. Jon Bon Jovi—classic rock, country rock, rock music, heavy metal, etc.

These rankings vary depending on which site one visits. For example, on imbd.com, the world's most popular and authoritative source for movie, television, and celebrity content and a subsidiary of Amazon.com since 1998, ranks Adam Levine number one; Jared Leto number two; Kurt Cobain number three; Gavin Rossdale number four; and Robin Thicke number five.

Source: https://www.imdb.com/list/ls053562999/ ,

https://www.ranker.com/crowdranked-list/hottest-male-singers

Ranker is a leading digital media company for opinion-based, crowd sourced rankings on just about everything

The Most Attractive Female Pop Stars

1. Shakira – pop star famous for hits like "Whenever, Whenever" and "Hips Don't Lie".
2. Katy Perry- pop, rock, disco and gospel music star.
3. Camila Cabello- pop, R&B, and Latin influenced rising star famously known for "Havana".
4. Ariana Grande- pop, R&B and disco. She's also an actress.
5. Selena Gomez—She's an experienced fashion designer and a young promising Hollywood star

Websites like webvisible.com, name Beyoncé Knowles as number one; Shakira, number two; Avril Lavigne, number three; Katy Perry, number four; and Mariah Carey, number five.

There are many beautiful female music artists on the American scene, but we cannot list them all in this one book.

Source: https://webvisible.com/hottest-female-singers-id=2665/ , https://www.ranker.com/crowdranked-list/the-25-sexiest-women-in-pop-music

Now that we've come to know the greatest songs of all time on America's Billboard Chart, and the celebrity musicians we all enjoy listening to, let's catch up where we left off on our on-going topic of American Culture.

Trending today is the booming business of **e-commerce** with the internet and the ability to purchase any type of product within the comfort of one's home and with the mere press of a button on a computer, tablet, or phone.

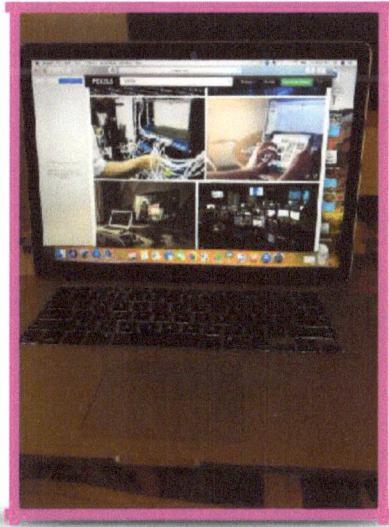

Business on the Internet

We cannot forget the powerful **Media and Entertainment** Industries in America that have had a massive impact and influence around the world. It is said that the U.S. houses ⅓ of the world's media and entertainment industry. At $735 billion, the Media and Entertainment Industry is expected to grow to $830 billion by 2022, according to the latest projections from Price Waterhouse Coopers (PWC).

Source: https://www.selectusa.gov/media-entertainment-industry-united-states

America is known for its **television** programming which started in 1945 by National Broadcasting Company (NBC) and the **movie** industry based in Hollywood, California. NBC was founded in 1927 under the name National Broadcast Company. They became the first television company to begin regularly scheduled television network service in the United States. The first television station to begin broadcasting in analog television signals was W2XB, the forerunner to WRGB in 1928, in Schenectady, New York.

New York, the biggest city in America, is the home of Broadway and a specialty area for theatrical and folk arts.

Source: https://en.wikipedia.org/wiki/List_of_years_in_television

America is also known for its **football, baseball, basketball,** and **hockey.** While baseball has been America's favorite past time for a long time, it has been overtaken by football in popularity in the last three decades.

Other sports of great importance in America include horse racing, wrestling, ice hockey, golf, auto racing, volleyball, skateboarding, snowboarding, and athletic games at the Olympic stage that have made the United States a power house by winning 2,522 medals at the summer Olympic games, more than any other country, and 281 in the winter Olympic games.

Boxing used to be very popular in America in the 1960's,70's and then again in the 1980's and 90's. Boxing figures like Muhammad Ali, George Foreman, Mike Tyson, Riddick Bowe, and Jack Johnson the first African American Heavy Weight Champion (1908-1915), made headlines the world over.

According to Wikipedia, the free encyclopedia, John L. Sullivan became the first American heavyweight champion in 1882 under bare knuckle boxing rules and again in 1892 in the first gloved era. He was defeated by James Corbett, the man often referred to as the father of modern boxing in 1892 due to his innovative scientific technique in 1892.

However, the sport declined in the late 1990's due among other factors to the lack of a U.S. heavy weight world champion and lack of main stream coverage in the newspapers and major television networks. It was hoped that the Floyd Mayweather Jr. vs Manny Pacquiao fight in 2015 would rekindle the interest in the sport, but because the fight was perceived as disappointing, promoters believed the sport was doing further harm than good in the United States.

Source: https://en.wikipedia.org/wiki/History_of_sports_in_the_ United_States , https://www.marintheatre.org/productions/fetch-clay-make-man/fcmm-boxing , https://en.wikipedia.org/wiki/Boxing_in_ the_United_States

American **architecture** is as diverse as its multi-cultural society and represents a variety of styles and forms. It is innovative, eclectic, and has visible traces of influence by the British and Spanish rule over the last four centuries.

Victorian Architecture (johngarzon.com)

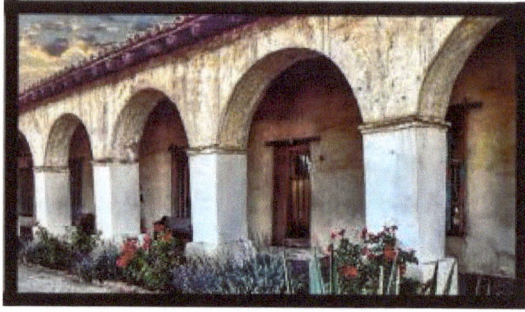

Spanish Colonial (dunnedwards.com)

The architectural styles and influences include, among others, colonial architecture for a new nation, mid-19th century, pre-Columbian, and revivalism in the 20th century. Some types of architecture are Georgian, Spanish, English, American Colonial, Greek revival, Spanish Colonial revival, Gothic revival, American Foursquare, Shingle style architecture, International Style and Federal Architecture.

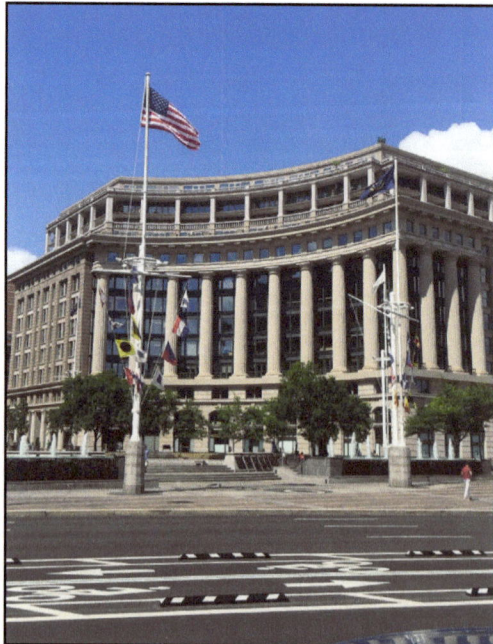

Federal Architecture Building

Federal Architecture Style

Georgian Architecture

Photo source: https://free-images.com/lg/0b45/lytham_hall_lytham_saint.jpg

The style Moderne and the Interwar Skyscraper brought skyscrapers notably into existence when they were built in New York from 1913.

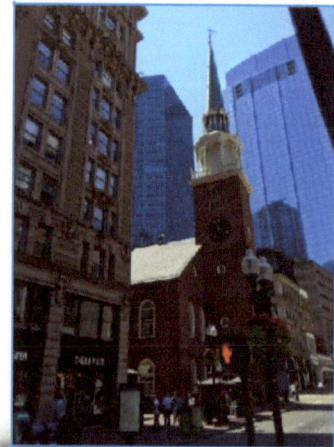

Moderne Architecture (archive photo)
Skyscrapers in Boston
(archive photo)

Finally, the American culture topic cannot conclude without mentioning the **holidays** that are celebrated only in America where millions of people look forward to them.

HOLIDAYS	THE CELE-BRATION
Martin Luther King Junior (3rd Monday, January)	Celebration of the Civil Rights Leader Martin Luther King Jr.
President's Day (3rd Monday, February)	Celebration of presidents George
	Washington and Abraham Lincoln.
Memorial Day (Last Monday in May)	A day to remember the fallen military service men &
	women.
July 4	Independence Day

Labor Day (1st Monday, September)	A day to commemorate the American workforce and its achieve-ments.
Thanksgiving (4th Thursday, November)	A celebration of the harvest and peoples' successes.
Veteran's Day (11 November)	A celebration of America's surviving War Veterans.

7

GREAT ATTRACTIONS IN THE U.S.

Grand Prismatic Spring (Photo by: Grant Ordelheide)

These are the places you must see in America before you run out of money or get tangled up in the workaholic life-style of this country.

1. The **Grand Prismatic Spring** in Yellowstone National Park, Wyoming is the largest hot spring in the U.S. and the third largest in the world, behind New Zealand's Frying Pan Lake and the Boiling Lake in Dominican Republic.

2. **Watkins Glen State Park**-Finger Lakes State Park, New York. Watkins is a 400-foot deep gorge with breathtaking waterfalls and scenic views.

Watkins Glen State Park

Fly Geyser

3. **Fly Geyser**

Nevada. One might think this is a rock tulip bursting with red and greenish leaves to expose a mystic formation of a structure that leaves you dumbstruck.

Source: https://upload.wikimedia.org/wikipedia/commons/4/41/ Fly_geyser.jpg

The Wave

Photo by: (https://en.wikipedia.org/wiki/The_Wave,_Arizona)

4. **The Wave**, Arizona. This is a rock, eroded by wind for millions and millions of years in the Paris Canyon/Vermilion Cliff Wilderness of Arizona. The Navajo sandstone is a work of nature that simply blows your mind.

5. **The Northern Lights**, Alaska. These lights are heavenly and lack the proper words to describe them. You must visit to believe for yourself. They are best seen in Fairbanks or Anchorage from September to April 20.

Northern Lights (photo by: https://cdn.pixabay.com/photo/2012/ 12/09/05/09/alaska-69135_1280.jpg)

Known as aurora borealis in the northern hemisphere and aurora australis in the southern hemisphere, the Northern Lights are formed as a result of collisions between gaseous particles in the earth's atmosphere with charged particles released from the sun's atmosphere. The heated particles—electrons and protons—are blown and carried to the earth's atmosphere by solar wind. The collision with gas particles in the earth's atmosphere leads to the emission of light that is understood to be the dancing lights of the north.

The color that is commonly seen is a pale yellowish-green produced by oxygen molecules. Nitrogen, a colorless and odorless unreactive gas, produces blue and purplish-red aurora, whereas the rare all-red auroras are produced by high-altitude oxygen.

6. **Horsetail Fall, Yosemite National Park**, California. This is a seasonal waterfall that flows in the winter and early spring. The waterfall glows orange and red when the setting sun illuminates it in February of every year when weather conditions are favorable. Horsetail Fall occurs on the east side of El Capitan (a vertical rock formation in Yosemite National Park), located on the north side of Yosemite Valley.

Horsetail Falls

Source: https://www.world-of-waterfalls.com/images/Horsetail_Falls _13_ns_016L.jpg ,

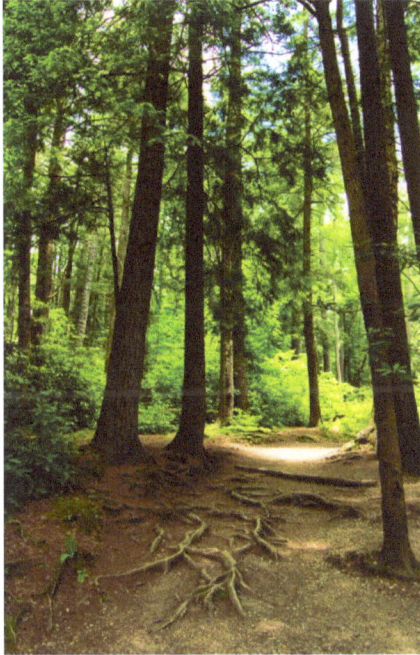

Blue Ridge Parkway (photo by: Alex Armstrong)
Photo courtesy of Julie and Johnny.

7. **Blue Ridge Parkway**, Virginia and North Carolina. This is America's longest linear park. It is miles and has 360 miles of hiking, 13 picnic areas, biking trails, music festivals, and several camping grounds.

8. **Sequoia National Park**, California. It is said you will feel like a dwarf—a small person—before these huge trees. The biggest is 2,500 years old, stands at 275 feet tall, and is the largest living tree in the world called the General Sherman Tree.

General Sherman Tree (photo by: https://www.nps.gov/seki/planyour visit/sequoiagroves.htm)

Maine Lighthouses
(Archive photo)-Portland

9. **Maine Lighthouses**, Portland, Maine. There are six of these lighthouses, about 20 minutes' drive from each other. They offer knowledge into the maritime location and provide a rich history of thecity of Portland.

10. **The Great Lakes**: Lake Michigan, Lake Superior, Lake Huron, Lake Ontario and Lake Erie. These are the largest group of fresh water lakes. It's amazing to catch a bird's eye view of the lakes and to see the surrounding landscape which is teaming with wildlife.

https://upload.wikimedia.org/wikipedia/commons/5/57/Great_Lakes_from_space_crop_labeled.jpg ,

11. **Niagara Falls**, New York. These falls blow you away. From the distant scenic view of them to the close-up of the cloudy white-water falls roaring with foams of mist beating over rugged rocks in the background, makes the Niagara Falls look spectacular with a touch of fearsomeness.

Niagara Falls

Photo by: New York States Office of Parks

12. **Skagit Valley Tulip Field,** Washington. These flowers are imposingly beautiful. They remind me of thousands and thousands of military police dressed in red tops (hats) at a parade waiting to be inspected. The tulips bloom in April and create a beautiful view with the mountains in the background.

Photo by: pexels.com

8

EDUCATION IN AMERICA: THE AMERICAN EDUCATION SYSTEM

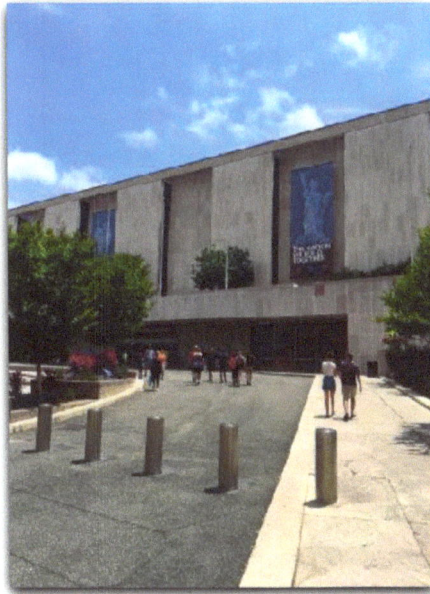

Archive photo: **Museum of American History** (Washington D.C.)

Education in the U.S, follows the Primary, Secondary, College/University structure.

The difference between this education system and other education systems in most countries is that it's called different names at the primary/secondary levels and its more open and flexible at the higher or tertiary level.

Archive Photo: **An Exhibit at the National Air and Space Museum**
(Washington D.C)

Typically, a child will begin formal school in kindergarten at age 5 or 6 and go through elementary school, first grade-sixth grade. At age 11 or 12, the student enters secondary school which is divided into two stages: middle school/junior high which consists of 7th through 9th grade and high school, consisting of 10th through 12th grade. Students normally take 6 years to complete this stage, spending 3 years in middle school and 3 years in high school.

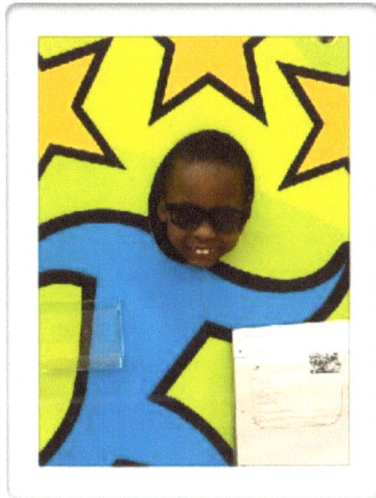

There are variations to the 6-3-3 structure at the school level. Some school districts have 5-3-4, 6-2-4 structure, while others—mostly small/rural and some private ones—use the structure of elementary as K-8th grade and High School as 9th -12th grade. In the first 6 years of a student's life at school, they will have one teacher for all the major subjects studied, but after sixth grade they will have a teacher for each subject they take.

This stands out, quite different from other countries where students have a teacher for every subject undertaken, right from their first years in primary school. Such countries include but are not limited to Uganda and Kenya in East Africa, the United Kingdom, Australia, South Korea, Germany, and Singapore.

Public education in America is free and compulsory and all school-going children must attend school, either at a public institution, private, or at home (homeschooling). Before kindergarten, children are encouraged to attend preschool to prepare them for the years ahead.

At the end of the twelve grades in school, students graduate with either a diploma or certificate.

Museum of Science
(Boston)

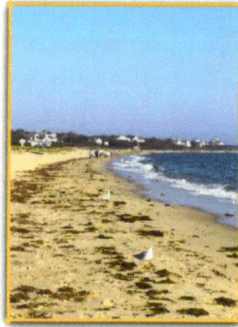

One of the Beaches
at Cape Cod

Somewhere
in the Wild

Thousands of school children go the Museum of Science in Boston every year to learn about animal and plant life and the new innovations and inventions in science. This museum includes exhibits on the study of plants, animals, bird life, and aquatic life, without forgetting the interesting subject of the planets in the universe, making science an essential part of the children's education and appreciation of the environment around them.

At age 17 or 18, students often go to college or university to receive higher education. The school calendar begins in August or September and ends in May or June. The academic year begins in autumn.

One year of school consists of two semesters in a year for college or university and these are divided into either a 3-term (trimester) system or 4-term system. The summer session is optional.

U.S. HIGHER EDUCATION SYSTEM

To pursue higher education in the United States, students undergo three levels of education: the **Undergraduate**, the **Graduate**, and **Graduate in pursuit of a Doctorate Degree**.

At the **undergraduate level**, students spend 4 years pursuing a bachelor's degree at a Community College or University/College. The first two years are spent studying a variety of subjects in different classes, pre-requisites to attaining a bachelor's degree. In the third academic year, students specialize in a "Major" subject, which becomes the specific field of study associated with the degree they will get. For example, a Bachelor of Arts (B.A.) in Business Administration or B.A. in Education.

Boeing Milestones of Flight Hall (Washington , D.C.)

Many students choose to spend their first two years of college or university at a Community College where they can attain an Associate of Arts (AA) Transfer Degree to a university or college. Some students might opt to stop at this level, settling for an Associate Degree to enter directly into the work force, while others may continue to finish their final two years at a university or college to obtain a higher degree.

The students who choose to stop at the Associate Degree level usually want to begin working immediately so as to start earning a living or pay off their college loan; many of these students do not have the funds to complete another two years at the university. Those who proceed to finish their four years and achieve an honors degree usually have the funds required to pay for their tuition or the job requirements of their specific field of specialization demands they get a degree. Students can change their "Majors" several times before finishing their bachelor's degree if they so wish. This explains the flexibility of higher education in America.

The second level of higher education is the **graduate** in pursuit of a Master's Degree. This level takes 2 years to complete. Not every profession requires someone to undertake a Master's Degree (MBA) but others do, like engineering and behavioral health if one is to achieve those higher positions of management.

To get an MBA, a student must prepare and complete a long research paper called a "Master Project" or "Master's Thesis".

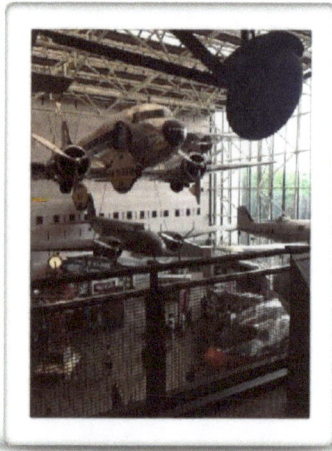

An exhibit at the National Air and Space Museum in Washington D.C. Archive photo.

The third level of higher education is the **graduate pursuing to get a Doctorate Degree.**

The Doctorate of Philosophy (PhD) degree takes home-based students (students within the U.S.) 3 years to complete, whereas it may takes 5 or 6 years for International students to complete. Students can directly prepare for a PhD without first acquiring a master's degree in the U.S.

Students pursuing a PhD are required to spend the first 2 years in classes and attending seminars where they exchange ideas and opinions on their specialized field of study; then they must spend one year doing first-hand research and writing theses or dissertations which they must publish. Their findings must be previously unpublished. Most universities and schools offering PhD's in the U.S. also require that such students have a reading knowledge of at least two foreign languages.

Higher education in America works on a credit-based system where students are recognized for having taken a course at a college or university. This measure is a determinant to attaining a degree of one's choice. Credits are the number of hours that a student spends in a class for a particular course in a week for one term or semester. Each week, students meet for three hours over a 15-week semester.

Each semester credit hour (SCH) equals 15-16 actual hours of study per semester which translates into 45 or 46 contact hours of study. Most courses in colleges and universities have a 3-semester credit hour. Students must complete a given number of credit hours to graduate. If a student changes colleges or universities before completing his/her degree program, the credits attained at the former university are transferred to the new university/college where he/she will finish the degree program.

(Library Photo courtesy of pexels.com)

International students pursuing a doctorate degree are considered full-time students when they enroll in any university in the United States and are required to study a minimum of 2 credits per semester. Occasionally, students are permitted to pursue a post-master's PhD on a part-time basis, but they must demonstrate a commitment to the program on an on-going basis. Undergraduates and students pursuing a master's degree can pursue their study either full-time or part-time.

Source: http://www.bu.edu/academics/eng/programs/doctoral-programs-overview/ ,

TYPES OF U.S. HIGHER EDUCATION

1. **State College or University**: This type of higher education is run by the State or Local Government. All 50 States in the U.S. have at least one State University and several State Colleges. These universities are public and most have the name of the State in their title. An example is UMASS Boston—the University of Massachusetts in Boston.

2. **Private Colleges or Universities**: These are often smaller in size than State universities. They usually charge higher tuition rates than State-run universities or colleges and are affiliated to religious organizations. They are privately owned and are open to students who

subscribe to other students who religious beliefs, they have the jurisdiction to admit students who do and do not profess the belief of the school's or college's founder.

3. **Community Colleges**: Students attend two years in these colleges and acquire a transferable Associate Degree or a Certificate. There are two primary tracks at this college: One is the academic transfer degree where a student continues to a 4-year college or university to complete their degree course. The second is the branch that prepares students to enter the workforce directly. Transfer degrees include Associates of Art degrees and Associates of Science degrees. Associates of Applied Science and Certificates of completion are not likely to be transferable.

4. **Institute of Technology Schools**: These are four-year science and technology schools that offer graduate programs and short-term certificate courses.

The United States is a huge destination of students the world over, who come to seek knowledge from the world's best universities and interact with the biggest minds and most intelligent students.

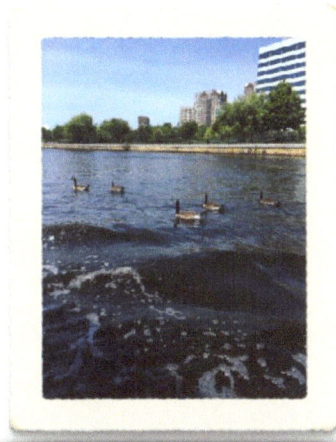

The City of Boston overlooks the Charles River

Boston, Massachusetts, is the number one destination of international students and students within the U.S. The Massachusetts Institute of Technology (MIT) established in 1861 and Harvard University established in 1638 rank 1st and 2nd in the best universities to attend in the U.S.

This is according to the QS World University

Rankings of 2015/16 (www.topuniversities.com). Boston also boasts of the first free publicly funded lending library in the U.S., the Boston Public Library founded in 1852 and located on 700 Boylston Street in Boston and Tufts University, a private research university in Medford, Massachusetts, formed in the 1970's. Prior to its transformation, Tufts University was called Tufts College founded in 1852.

New York, also known as the "city that never sleeps", follows Boston with its music, fashion, and arts business. Columbia University and New York University are 22nd and 53rd respectively in the QS Rankings and are names to reckon with in the largest city in the U.S.A.

San Francisco in California is the third most effective city in the U.S. at attracting international students. Stanford University is 3rd and the University of California, Berkeley is 26th in the World Rankings, dominating higher learning education in the west of the country.

Chicago City in Illinois follows San Francisco in rank at 10th place and boasts of the University of Chicago and North Western University at 32nd. The city of Chicago is famous for its blues and jazz music.

The city of **Los Angeles** is known for its creative industry—primarily music, television, and film—and is home to the University of California, Los Angeles (UCLA) which ranked 27th in the QS World University Rankings of 2015/16.

Washington, D.C. prides itself on the University of Maryland, College Park which topped at 126th in the QS Rankings. Students who study in the city can study and see for themselves the history and politics of the United States of America.

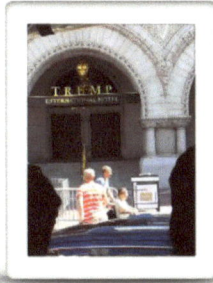

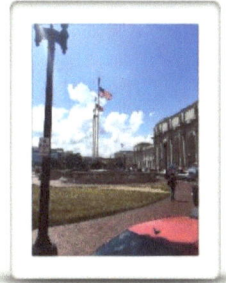

Displayed at the Holocaust Museum in Washington D.C
Sites of Washington DC
(Archive Photos)

The White House, U.S. Supreme Court, and many monuments and historical institutions are some of the must-see tourist sites for students who study and live in Washington, D.C.

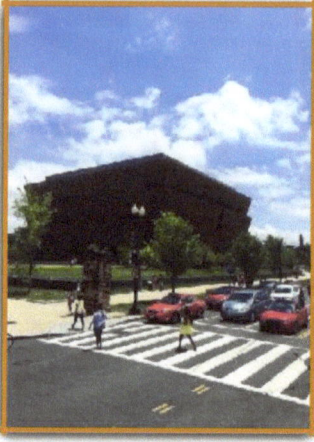

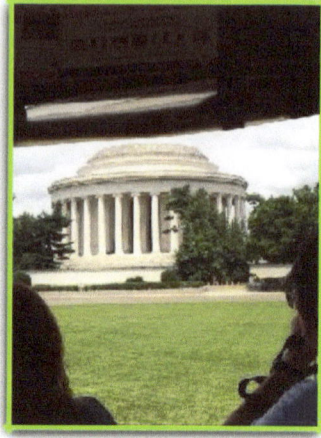

**Thomas Jefferson Memorial & The
African American Museum in
Washington D.C.**
(Archive photos)

9

INVENTIONS AND DISCOVERIES

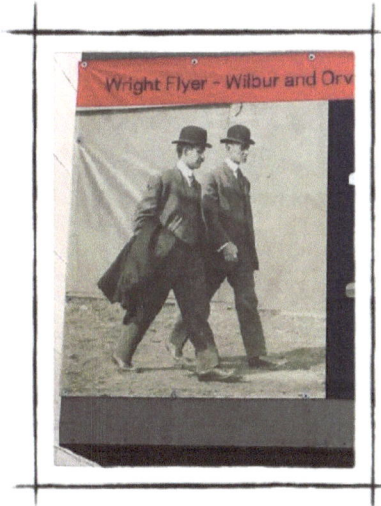

Wilber and Orville Wright Brothers Exhibit (On the steps to the Washington D.C. National Air and Space Museum) Archive photo.

In the field of discovery and inventions, the U.S. is a power house of personalities who have had and continue to have an impact on the world in terms of discoveries and inventions.

From the early seventeenth century to as recent as June 19, 2018, the United States Patent and Trade Marks Office has granted 10 million patents to Americans for the manufacture or creation of well-known inventions.

This book cannot compile all the wonderful discoveries made by native-born and naturalized citizens of this country. However, an effort is made here to highlight some of the most important discoveries and innovations.

In 1641, Samuel Winslow received the very first patent in North America when he discovered a **new method of making salt**. The patent was issued by the General Court of Massachusetts. Samuel Hopkins from Pittsford, Vermont was the first person in the U.S. to file and be granted a patent for his improved method of "**Making Pot and Pearl Ashes**" on July 31, 1790.

Benjamin Franklin, one of the founding Fathers of the United States of America, invented the **Swim Fins** (1717), Mail Order (1744), **Lightning Rod** (1749), **Flexible Urinary Catheter** (1752), and **Bifocals** in the early 1760's. Benjamin Franklin was an author, scientist, inventor, statesman, and diplomat as well.

Modern Swivel Chair (Archive photo)

The **Swivel Chair** or revolving chair which is famous in modern day offices, was invented by Thomas Jefferson in 1776.

Thomas Jefferson was a Founding Father of the U.S. He was also the principle author of the Declaration of Independence. He went on to become the third President of the United States of America from

1801 to 1809. In 1795, Thomas Jefferson invented the **Wheel Cypher**or the Jefferson disk—a cipher system for encrypting messages and used as a deterrent for codebreaking.

Cupcakes were baked as early as 1796 and referenced in a recipe book "American Cookery" by Amelia Simms. The world's first **suspension bridge**, the Jacob's Creek Bridge, was invented by James Finley of Uniontown, Pennsylvania in 1801.

In 1805, Oliver Evans invented an **amphibious vehicle**, a type of vehicle that can be used on both land and water. The **Coffee Percolator**, a kind of pot used to brew coffee, was invented by Benjamin Thompson Rumford in 1806.

Dental Floss, a type of plastic ribbon or bundle of thin nylon filaments used to remove food particles from teeth was invented by Levi Spear Parmly, a dentist from New Orleans in 1815.

The **electric door** bell was the brain child of Joseph Henry in 1831. The **sewing machine** which sews clothes using the lockstitch technique was invented by an American called Walter Hunt in 1833.

Combine Harvester
Photo by: https://cdn.pixabay.com/photo/2016/08/02/13/18/combine-harvester-1563394_1280.jpg

The **Combine Harvester,** a type of machine that blends the jobs of harvesting, threshing, and cleaning up of grain crops was invented in 1834 by Hiram Moore.

The **Circuit Breaker,** an automatic switch that protects an electrical circuit from damage due to overload or short circuit was invented by Charles Grafton Page in 1836.

The **Sleeping Car,** a railroad passenger car that people sleep in at night while traveling, was the invention of Cumberland Valley Railroad in Pennsylvania in 1831 but it became commercially viable in 1857 when George Pullman invented the Pullman Sleeping Car.

New England housewife Nancy Johnson was the first American to invent a **hand-cranked ice-cream churn** in 1843.

Alexander Cartwright is credited for inventing the modern **sport of baseball** in 1845 when he wrote the official and codified set of regulated rules known as the Knickerbocker Rules.

The **gas mask** was invented in 1847 by Lewis Haslett. The **jackhammer** was an invention of Jonathan J. Couch from Pennsylvania. The **dishwasher** was invented in 1850 by Joel Houghton of Ogden, New York. The first dishwasher was a wooden one. The first successful dishwasher was invented by Josephine Cochrane in 1886.

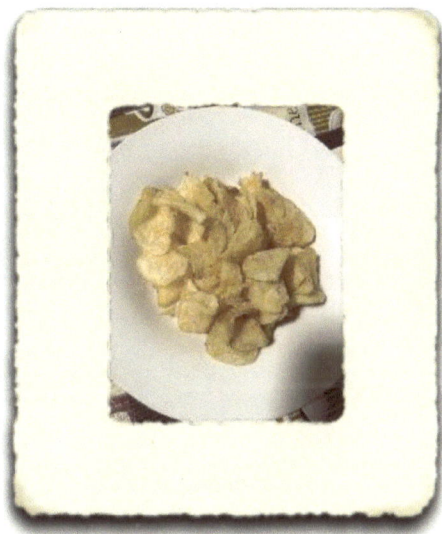

Potato Chips

Potato chips were first made by Chef George Crum, in New York in 1853. **Toilet Paper** was an invention of Joseph Gayetty in 1857, but since his toilet papers failed to take off, two brothers—Clarence and E. Irvin Scott of the Scott Paper Company—co-invented toilet rolls in 1890.

Gayetty's toilet paper was not successful because during the 19th century, it was taboo to openly discuss bathroom hygiene and, secondly, because Americans grew accustomed to wiping with the Sears Roebuck catalog which came in the mail free of charge; therefore, they saw no need to spend money on toilet paper.

In 1858, the **Ironing Board** was invented by investors William Vandenburg and James Harvey of New York City. The **escalator** was invented in 1859 by Nathan Ames from Saugus, Massachusetts. He called it the Revolving Stairs. The **machine gun** was invented by Richard Gatling in 1861. The **cowboy hat** was an invention of John Patterson Stetson during a hunting trip in 1865.

Phonograph

The **first vibrator** was invented by American physician George Taylor in 1869; it was powered by steam. The **Phonograph** or record player or gramophone was invented in 1877 by Thomas Alva Edison in New Jersey. A gramophone records, reproduces, and plays back sound.

Solar Cells which convert light energy into electrical energy were an invention of Charles Fritts in 1883. The account is from Encyclopedia Britannica. The **Skyscraper**, an impressive architecture type was designed and invented by William Le Baron Jenney, a Massachusetts born architect.

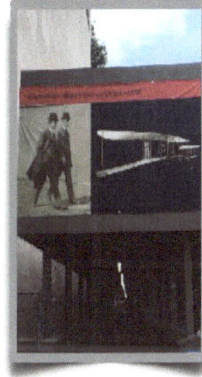

The Ferris Wheel   Wilber and Orville Wright Brothers" Archive photo.

Ballpoint Pen

The **ballpoint pen** is an invention of John Loud from Weymouth, Massachusetts in 1888. In 1891, George Washington Gale Ferris Jr. from Pittsburg, Pennsylvania invented the **Ferris Wheel**, a non-building structure that consists of an upright wheel with passenger gondolas attached to the rim.

Fast tracking into the 1900s, Ransom Olds created the **first Assembly line** in 1901. King Camp Gillette from Fond du Lac in Wisconsin, invented the **double-edged Safety razor** in 1901.

In 1902, Willis Haviland Carrier, a native of Angola, New York, invented and manufactured the first **mechanical air conditioning unit.**

The first **aircraft** was invented by the Wright Brothers, Wilbur and Orville Wright of Dayton, Ohio, in 1903.

Road Surface Marking was first done by Edward N. Hines in 1911. He originated the concept of separating traffic in opposite directions by painting a line down the center of the road. They were first used in Wayne County, Michigan. Policeman Lester Wire of Salt Lake City in Utah invented the first **traffic lights** in 1912. **Supermarkets** were an invention of Clarence Saunders with his Piggly Wiggly Stores in 1916. His first store opened in Memphis, Tennessee.

The **Polygraph** or lie detector was invented in 1921 by John Augustus Larson, a medical student at the University of California (Berkeley) and a police officer of the Berkeley Police Department in Berkeley, California.

The Bulldozer

The **Bulldozer,** a tractor that pushes large quantities of soil during construction, was designed by a farmer in Morrowville, Kansas named James Cummings and a draftsman Earl J. McLeod in 1923.

In the same year, the **Instant Camera**—a camera with self-developing film—was invented by Samuel Shlafrock from the County of Bronx, New York. In 1926, Dr. Robert H. Goddard from Auburn Massachusetts, launched the first **liquid-fueled rocket** in the world. **Sunglasses** were first invented in 1929 by Sam Foster, founder of Foster Grant, an American brand of eyewear. The first pair of Foster Grant sunglasses were sold on the Boardwalk in Atlantic City, New Jersey.

The **Tiltrotor**, a type of aircraft that uses a pair of rotors mounted on rotating shafts at the end of a fixed wing for purposes of lifting the aircraft was invented in 1930 by George Lehberger of Union Township, Hudson County, New Jersey.

Electric Guitar

The **electric guitar** was invented in 1931 by George Beauchamp and Adolph Rickenbacker. Together with Paul Barth, the trio formed Ro-Pat-In Company which produced and sold electrified instruments. Gorge Beauchamp lived in Los Angeles, while Adolph Rickenbacker lived in Orange County, California.
Photo by : https://upload.wikimedia.org/wikipedia/commons/f/fc/Ibanez_ Studio_ST-370_electric_guitar_body.jpg

George Inman, an employee at General Electric's Nela Park facility in Cleveland, Ohio, invented the **Compact Fluorescent Lamp** in

1936. The patent for the invention was issued to him on October 14, 1941. In 1937, George Robert Stibitz built the world's first **relay-based computer** while working at Bell Telephone Laboratories in New York City. He is recognized the world over as the father of the modern digital computer.

The **Automated Teller Machine** (ATM) was invented in 1939 by Luther George Simjian, an Armenian-American in New York City. The **microwave** oven is an invention of Percy Spencer in 1945. He was an American physicist and inventor who worked for Raytheon Company, a major U.S. defense contractor and industrial corporation by the time he invented the microwave.

Microwave Oven (Archive Photo)

1947 saw the manufacture and operationalization of the first **Supersonic Aircraft** in the U.S. The Bell X-1 aircraft was piloted by Air-Force Captain Chuck Yeager who became the first pilot to have exceeded the speed of sound in level flight.

Supersonic Aircraft

https://images.pexels.com/photos/80455/delta-wings-aircraft
-stealth-bomber-cloak-of-invisibility-80455.jpeg?auto=compress&cs
=tinysrgb&dpr=2&h=350

Cable television was started by John Walson and Margaret Walson in the mountains of Pennsylvania in 1948.

Hubert Schlafly invented the **teleprompter** in 1950 while working at Century Fox film studios in Los Angeles, California. The **barcode** was invented in 1952. This is an optical machine-readable representation of data that is capable of reading information shown on certain products. It was invented by Norman Joseph Woodland while staying at his grandfather's apartment in Florida. He and Bernard Silver, fellows at Drexel Institute of technology based in Philadelphia, Pennsylvania, applied for a patent on October 20, 1949 and received it on October 7, 1952.

American physicist, Gordon Gould from New York City, is widely seen as the first inventor of **Laser** in 1957, a device that emits electro-magnetic radiation through a process called stimulation emission.

The John Hopkins University Applied Physics Laboratory located in Howard County, Maryland was the first body to develop and launch successfully a **Global Navigation Satellite System** (GNSS) in 1960 called Transit also known as NAVSAT or NNSS (Navy Navigation Satellite System). The system was primarily used by the U.S. Navy to provide accurate location information to its Polaris ballistic missile submarines and as a navigation system by the Navy's surface ships before it was opened to civilian use later.

Joe Sutter, the chief engineer of the Jumbo Jet program at Boeing in King County, Seattle, Washington designed the world's first **wide-body aircraft**, the BOEING 747 in 1969.

Boeing 747

Photo by: https://cdn.pixabay.com/photo/2016/10/25/04/13/jetliner-1767861__480.jpg

The first **personal computer** to be invented was called Kenbak-1 and was invented by John Blankenbaker of Kenbak Corporation in his garage in Los Angeles in 1970 and sold in early 1971.

Source: http://history-computer.com/ModernComputer/Personal/Kenbak-1.html, https://en.wikipedia.org/wiki/Kenbak-1

The **Global Positioning System** (GPS) is a space based GNSS system that was created in 1972 as a result of a collaborative team effort by Colonel Bradford Parkinson, Mel Birnbaum, Jim Spilker, and Bob Rennard. In 1973, it was approved and in 1978, the first GPS satellite was launched. The project was owned by the United States government and operated by the United States Air Force.

Motorola Phones

Motorola phones – source: https://cdn.pixabay.com/photo/2018/10/29/12/22/motorola-talkr-walk-n-talk-3781021__480.jpg

The first **handheld cellular/mobile phone** or cell phone was invented by Martin Cooper in 1973. At the time he invented the handheld mobile phone, he was the head of Motorola's communications system division in Schaumburg, Illinois.

The first **hand-held Digital Camera** was invented by Steven Sasson, an American electrical engineer at Eastman Kodak in Rochester, New York in 1975.

The **Lockheed F-117 Nighthawk** was the first operational aircraft to use stealth technology in 1981. Lockheed Advanced Development Projects was awarded a contract popularly known as the Skunk Works in Burbank, California by the United States Defense Advanced Research Projects Agency (DARPA) to build and test two stealth strike fighter jets. The F-117A made its maiden flight from Groom Lake, Nevada on June 18, 1981. The F-117A reached operational capability in October, 1983.

Nighthawk Aircraft

Photo   source: https://upload.wikimedia.org/wikipedia/commons/
thumb/a/a1/F-117_Nighthawk_Front.jpg/1599px-F-117_Night-
hawk_Front.jpg

The **Space Shuttle** was launched in 1981 as well, and George Muel-
ler from St. Louis, Missouri is widely credited for designing, overseeing,
and jumpstarting the space shuttle program after the end of the Apollo
program in 1972.

January 1, 1983 is considered the "birth" date of the **internet**. This
took place in the United States of America when the first Transmission
Control Protocol and Internet Protocol (TCP/IP) wide area network
was operational. This allowed different kinds of computers on different
networks to "talk" to each other. Before this, various computer networks
did not have a standard way to communicate with each other.

Prior to 1983, Bob Khan, a native of Brooklyn, New York, and Vin-
ton Cerf, a native of New Haven, Connecticut had co-invented the Internet Protocol and Transmission Control Protocol while working on
the world's first electronic computer network, the ARPANET (The
Advanced Research Projects Agency Network) in 1973 at the United
States Department of Defense. ARPANET (established in 1969) and
TCP/IP (1973) became the technical foundation technologies of the
internet.

Source : https://www.usg.edu/galileo/skills/unit07/internet07_02.phtml , https://en.wikipedia.org/wiki/ARPANET , https://en.wikipedia.org/wiki/Internet

The **Nicotine Patch,** used as a method to stop smoking, was invented in 1988 by Murray Jarvis, Daniel Rose, and Jed Rose at the University of California, Los Angeles. The **University of South California** was the first body to enter the field of **Deoxyribonucleic Acid** (DNA) Computing in 1994.

The **Nanowire battery** is a co-invention of Chinese-American Dr. Yi Cui and his colleagues at Stanford University in 2007. It is said that a nanowire battery can hold far more energy than a standard lithium-ion battery. Using a steel anode covered in silicon nanowires, the nanowire battery can ran a laptop computer for up to 20 hours non-stop, rather than the 2 hours of a regular lithium-ion battery.

2008 saw the creation of **Bionic Contact Lenses** by Iranian-American Babak Parviz, an electrical engineer at the University of Washington in Seattle. These are digital contact lens worn directly on the human eye. Scientists believe that in the future, they can serve as a useful virtual platform for monitoring a patient's medical condition among many other uses.

Joseph Marron of Manhattan Beach, California, was given patent number 10 million on June 19, 2018 for inventing a **frequency modulated or coherent laser detection and ranging system**. The system describes a method of bouncing lasers off targets to figure out their range and velocity. The system according to the U.S. Patent and Trademark Office (USPTO), can be applied to such varied fields as autonomous vehicles, military defense systems, medical imaging devices, and space and underwater exploration. Patent 10 million is, however, owned by Raytheon Company based in Waltham, Massachusetts.

Source: https://en.wikipedia.org/wiki/Timeline_of_United_States_inventions ,

https://en.wikipedia.org/wiki/Timeline_of_United_States_inventions_(1890–1945) , https://en.wikipedia.org/wiki/Timeline_of_United_States_inventions_(1946–91) ,

https://en.wikipedia.org/wiki/Timeline_of_United_States_inventions_(after_1991) ,

https://www.uspto.gov/about-us/news-updates/united-states-issues-patent-number-10000000 ,

10

THE BAD AND UGLY IN THE INNER CITIES OF AMERICA

The biggest heists and bank robberies in American History

1. On March 24th, 1972, Amill Dinsilo and a group of relatives plus alarm experts stole $30 million—equal to around $172.4 million today—from the United California Bank, Launga Niguel, California. Most of the money was recovered and the culprits were caught after police discovered fingerprints on unwashed dishes in the dishwasher of the townhouse said to be their headquarters.

2. Samuel Nalo and Robert Comfort have gone down in history for committing the "most successful hotel robbery" by stealing $27 million—equal to $155.2 million today—from Pierre Hotel, New York in 1972. They are listed in the Guinness World Records for pocketing that money.

3. The Dunbar Armored Car robbery has been named the largest cash robbery in the U.S. $18.9 million-equal to $28.3 million today-was stolen from the Dunbar Armored Facility, L.A. California by Allen Pace who had been a regional safety inspector of Dunbar. This happened on September 12th, 1997.

Pace was later convicted and sentenced to 24 years in prison, but some of the money has never been recovered to this day.

N.B: Some people go about in life trying to make a good name in a good way, but others will do the contrary at whatever cost. What will you choose?

Source: https://www.worldatlas.com/articles/biggest-heists-and-bank -robberies-in-american-history.html

11

WORLD VIEW OF AMERICA AND HOW AMERICA VIEWS THE WORLD

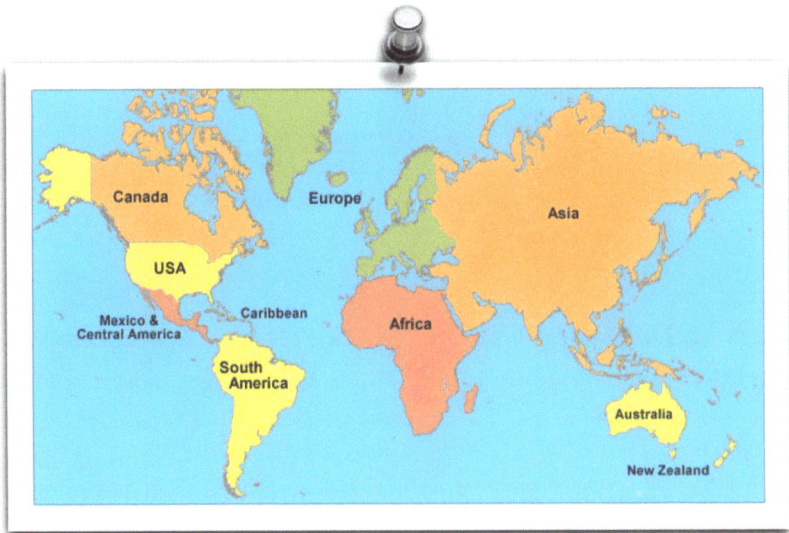

World Map
Source: https://geology.com/world/world-map-clickable.gif

The rest of the world has always viewed America as a "super-power" in terms of national military might and strength. That's why—up until now—countries and regions all over the globe run to it in need of help and protection to bolster their security against adversaries and to guarantee their continued existence in an uncertain and unpredictable world.

The United States of America is seen as the country of destination for many people who are looking for a better life or who want to turn around their lives/conditions. The U.S. is perceived to be a country where "dreams come true" and where "you can be what you want to be" if only you work hard at it.

Photo source: https://images.pexels.com/photos/853168/pexels-photo-853168.jpeg?auto=compress&cs=tinysrgb&dpr=2&h=650&w=940

For those who are persecuted and threatened in their home countries for speaking out against tyrannical and dictatorial regimes and governments, America is their number one destination. Why? Because America has had a long history of protecting people's freedoms.

In the U.S., freedom of speech, assembly, association, freedom of the press, and human rights are guaranteed and protected under its constitution. It's no wonder refugees and asylum seekers from all over the world seek the homage and protection of this great country.

Recent trends, however, in U.S. political life have made many people wonder whether the above values they hold about America are still unshakable. The election of President Donald Trump in 2016 and his campaign promises to stop Muslims from entering the United States in fear of Islamic terrorists attacking American citizens here at home, to building a wall at the southern border with Mexico to prevent illegal entrance of refugees and asylum seekers, combined with a lock up of his presidential campaign rival Hillary Clinton due to her misuse of a personal e-mail server to store sensitive national security information, have left many people feeling uncertain about the future of the country. Not to mention the constant attacks on the press and journalists as enemies of the people and accusations of them reporting fake news and attacking his personality and presidential policies. This left many people feeling unsure of their long held traditions and beliefs about the American people.

Music Mixer

America continues to be viewed as the dominant country in the music and entertainment world. Celebrities like Beyoncé, Christina Aguilera, Mariah Carey, Janet Jackson, Jennifer Lopez, Madonna, Britney Spears, Drake

Bell, Chris Brown, Michael Jackson, Justin Timberlake, Dr. Luke, Bobby Brown, Elvis Presley, Billy Joel, Whitney Houston, Kenny Rogers, and many other music icons including today's stars like Taylor Swift, Tim McGraw, R. Kelly, Jay Z, Lady Gaga, Ariana Grande, and Katy Perry have made their mark on the music industry world-wide.

R. Kelly

Lady Gaga

Jennifer Lopez

Justin Timberlake

Jay Z & Kanye West

Beyoncé

Ariana Grande

Tim McGraw

Taylor Swift

All celebrity photos courtesy of shutterstock.com

https://image.shutterstock.com/image-photo/los-angeles-feb-10-jennifer-450w-136598402.jpg , https://image.shutterstock.com/image-photo/venice-italy-august-31-lady-450w-1196414656.jpg , https://image.shutterstock.com/image-photo/r-kelly-performs-on-stage-450w-546085786.jpg , https://image.shutterstock.com/image-photo/las-vegas-may-20-taylor-450w-1097570879.jpg , https://image.shutterstock.com/image-photo/los-angeles-feb-10-faith-450w-1129097489.jpg , https://image.shutterstock.com/image-photo/ariana-grande-2016-american-music-450w-522342139.jpg , https://image.shutterstock.com/image-photo/los-angeles-feb-10-beyonce-450w-1129097909.jpg , https://image.shutterstock.com/z/stock-photo-kanye-west-and-jay-z-at-the-world-premiere-of-jay-z-s-fade-to-black-at-the-the-ziegfeld-theater-on-160850204.jpg , https://image.shutterstock.com/image-photo/cannes-france-may-11-justin-450w-732211825.jpg

The movie and entertainment business continue to be dominated by Hollywood and Disney in California. Movie companies and film studios by the names of Warner Brothers, 20th Century Fox, Paramount Pictures, Universal Pictures, Walt Disney Studio, and Sony Pictures Entertainment among a collection of movie companies have continued to make their imprint on Hollywood and the rest of the world with their blockbuster movies.

Video Camera

N.B: Let's take another break now and find out about the greatest American films ever made.

THE GREATEST AMERICAN FILMS OF ALL TIME

In this section I will mention only five of the greatest American movies and another five of the biggest blockbuster movies of all time. The last segment will be dedicated to the top five blockbuster movies that have brought in the biggest chunk of money in box office sales in the U.S.

This is an updated edition (10th edition) of the American Film Institute's (AFI) 100 Years … 100 Movies—a list of the top 100 greatest American films of all time. These films are nominated by 1,500 film artists, critics, and historians of the film community in America. The nomination takes place after every 10 years. As mentioned above, I will list only five of the 100 greatest movies. Since 2007, when the 10th edition list was released by the AFI, no current list of the 20th edition has been released yet. It was supposed to be released in 2017.

1. Citizen Kane (1941) —Drama.
2. The Godfather (1972) —Drama.
3. Casablanca (1942) —Romance.
4. Raging Bull (1980) —Biography.
5. Singing in the Rain (1952)—Musical comedy.

The greatness of these movies is determined by their feature length, which must be 60 minutes or more, their popularity over time, critical recognition, major award winner status, and it must be an American movie made and filmed in the United States.

The movies below brought in the **highest film revenues worldwide of all time** according to IMDb, the world's most popular and authoritative source for movies, television, and celebrity content; The Numbers, a website where data and the movie business meet; and Newsday.com.

Figures for worldwide and domestic movie sales adjusted for ticket price inflation as of November 2018.

1. "Avatar" (2009) —$2.788 billion- Science Fiction.
2. "Titanic" (1997) —$2.187 billion- A Romance and Disaster film.
3. "Star Wars: The force Awakens" (2015) —$2.068 billion- Science Fiction and Fantasy film.
4. "Avengers: Infinity War" (2018) —$2.046 billion- A Superhero Adventure and Science fiction film.
5. "Jurassic World" (2015) —$1.671 billion- A Science Fiction and Adventure film.

TOP U.S. GROSSING DOMESTIC FEATURE FILMS

1. "Gone with the Wind" (1939) —$1.846 billion; a historical epic.
2. "Star Wars" (1977)—$1.628 billion; a science-fiction fantasy film.
3. "The Sound of Music" (1965) —$1.301 billion; a musical
4. "E.T: The Extra-Terrestrial" (1982) —$1.296 billion; a family adventure film.
5. "Titanic" (1997)—$1.238 billion; a romance and drama movie.

Source: https://www.boxofficemojo.com/alltime/world/ , https://www.newsday.com/entertainment/movies/the-biggest-box-office-hits-of-all-time-1.5369007 , https://www.filmsite.org/boxoffice.html

This country is also famous for its science, technology, and innovation prowess, especially in its space exploration and higher technology research and innovation. The center for this ingenuity and manufacturing is in **Silicon Valley** (SV), a region in the southern San Francisco Bay Area of Northern California. This is the region where, for example, the microprocessor and microcomputer were developed.

Silicon Valley is home to many of the world's largest high-tech corporations and start-up companies; companies like Tesla Motors, Apple, Hewlett Packard, AT&T, Google, Face Facebook, Wells Fargo, Visa the payment giant, Chevron the Pacific Coast oil giant, Oracle the software and cloud computing mega company, Intel the major manufacturer of computer parts, Cisco Systems the major company that brings information technology and telecommunication together, and NASA Ames Research Center have their headquarters in Silicon Valley.

Talking about Silicon Valley has reminded me of the people who have benefited from these startup tech companies and become billionaires themselves. So, without further ado, here are the five richest men and women in the United States of America as of October 2018. This list comes from the 2018 Forbes 400 Net Worth and from Time.com.

THE RICHEST MEN IN AMERICA

1. Jeff Bezos—CEO of Amazon.com. Net worth: $160 billion. He recently became the richest person in history. He started his company in his garage in Seattle, Washington in 1994.
2. Bill Gates—Co-Founder of Microsoft in 1975. He is 62 and his net worth is $97 billion. He made his money from the shares of his company after failing out of Harvard. He is from Seattle, Washington.
3. Warren Buffet—Age 87, he is the Chairman and CEO of Berkshire Hathaway, an investment firm. He is the only richest person in America who made his money from a field other than technology. It is said that he bought his first stock at age 11 and at age 13 he filed his first tax return with a $35 deduction for his bicycle. His net worth is $88.3 billion.
4. Mark Zuckerberg—Co-founder and Chairman of Facebook. Net worth: $61 billion. He is a Harvard dropout and started his own

company. He is 33 years old. Facebook is the largest social media network in the world.

5. Larry Ellison—Co-founder of Oracle and Chairman and Chief Technology Officer (CTO) of the same company. Oracle specializes in developing and marketing customer relationship management database software and technology. His net worth: $58.4 billion. He is 74.

THE RICHEST WOMEN IN AMERICA

1. Alice Walton—Heiress of the Wal-Mart fortune left behind by her father and Wal-Mart founder Sam Walton. Her net worth: $44.9 billion. She ranks number 12 on Forbes 2018 400. Wal-Mart is the largest private employer in the U.S. The Walton family foundation which Alice Walton runs with her family focuses on investing in K-12 education programs, environmental conservation, and improving the quality of life in Arkansas. She is 68.

2. Jacqueline Mars—Owner of Mars Inc. She ranks number 18 on Forbes 2018 400 of the Wealthiest Americans. Net worth: $24 billion. She also comes from one of America's richest families. Mars Inc., founded in 1911, is the largest maker of candy in the world. Brands include snickers, skittles, and M&Ms. She is 78.

3. Lauren Powell Jobs—Founder of the Emerson Collective, an organization that works with policy makers to create solutions to issues in education and immigration reform, among other social justice issues. She is the widow of Apple co-founder Steve Jobs. Steve Jobs died in 2011 and had a net worth of $11 billion before he passed on. Net worth of Lauren Powell Jobs: $20.5 billion. She ranks number 20 on the 2018 Forbes list of wealthiest Americans. She is 54.

4. Abigail Johnson—President and CEO of Fidelity Investment, a money management company. Net worth: $17.3 billion. Her grandfather founded the company in 1946. She features on the

Forbes 2018 list as number 28. She is 57 years old.

5.   Blair Parry-Okeden—Inherited a 25% stake in Cox Enterprises after the death of her mother Barbara Cox Anthony in 2007. Aged 67, Parry-Okeden is the daughter of James M. Cox who founded Cox Enterprise in 1898. The company specializes in communications and automotive services and is based in Atlanta, Georgia. Net worth: $9.3 billion. She ranks number 52 on the 2018 Forbes 400 Net Worth.

Source: http://time.com/money/5095574/the-10-richest-people-in-america/ , https://www.forbes.com/forbes-400/#577d19257e2f , http://time.com/money/5096770/richest-women-in-america/ ,

Who is the youngest billionaire in the U.S. according to Forbes? Snapchat co-founder Evan Spiegel is once again the youngest billionaire at age 28, according to the 2018 Forbes 400 wealthiest Americans. As of October 2018, Evan Spiegel's net worth was $2.3 billion and he ranked number 354 on the list. The second youngest billionaire is his partner, Bobby Murphy, age 30 who is also the co-founder of Snapchat. He is worth $2.3 billion as well. They have been at the top of the list of youngest billionaires since 2014.

Source: https://www.forbes.com/profile/evan-spiegel/?list=forbes-400#1dd 1ffb5529c,https://www.forbes.com/profile/bobby-murphy/?list=forbes-400# 3763784b37ba

Teaser
Answer

HOW AMERICA VIEWS THE WORLD

The United States of America views the world through the eyes of its foreign policy goals and decisions. The goal of U.S. foreign policy is to build and sustain a more democratic, secure, and prosperous world for the benefit of the American people and the international community. (Foreign Policy Agenda of the Department of State)

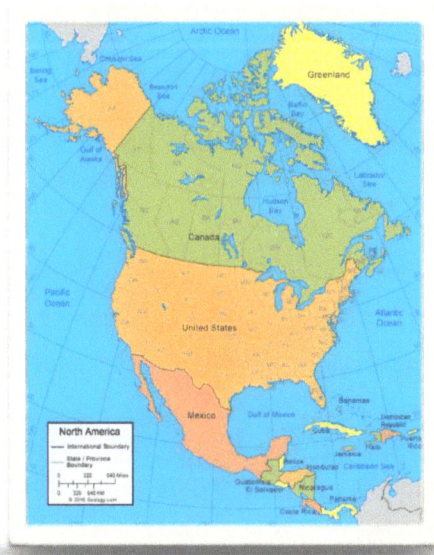

Map of U.S. in North America

The driving force behind the United State's outlook of the world has always been and remains to secure the country's political, economic, military, ideological, and humanitarian needs. For instance, the U.S. signs treaties and agreements with other nations to protect its existence and assure the safety of its allies. Negotiating treaties also helps to end regional conflicts. The U.S. signs trade deals with countries to promote U.S. trade and offer jobs to its citizens.

For decades, the United States has seen itself as the world's watch dog, protector, problem solver, and upholder of democratic principles and practices. In this respect, U.S. foreign policy favors nations that practice and promote democracy. Sometimes, however, due to conflicting goals with the country's national security, economics, or the realities of international politics, the U.S. has supported dictatorial governments in Africa, South America, and in the Middle East—or intervened to stop the emergence and rising of popular political movements in the world.

Flight Ware at the National Air and Space Museum, Washington D.C.
(Archive Photo).

It is part of U.S. foreign policy to promote peacekeeping in unstable regions, provide Foreign Aid to countries in need of help, and disaster relief to countries affected by war, natural disasters, or calamities.

Map of Africa

In line with the above, the United States has for decades been at the forefront of addressing economic and environmental problems in the world that would otherwise have an impact on its citizens both abroad and within the country.

Although U.S. policy has been changing since the Revolutionary War, through the nineteenth century, the two World Wars (WWI & WWII), the Great Depression of the 1930's, through the long, uncertain Cold War and now during the reign of President Trump, what has remained constant is the self-preservation and focus on the needs of the American people.

America's view of the world has been and continues to be determined and shaped by the U.S. President, Executive Branch, U.S. State Department, Senate, National Security Council, Congress, Supreme Court, and finally, the citizens themselves with special interest lobby groups. The strength and might of the United States of America is in its people or citizens, and the belief in its constitution and founding principles of liberty, equality, the pursuit of happiness, and the belief that all political power comes from the people.

Source: http://www.crf-usa.org/war-in-iraq/foreign-policy.html

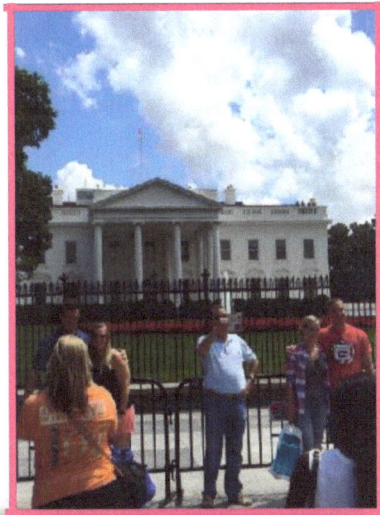

The White House

The power of the government and rights of citizens and all legal residents of this great country is today being questioned and tested by people both within and outside the U.S.

"The U.S. is less admired, less respected, and less feared than it needs to be", says Aaron David Miller, Middle East Adviser to former Democratic and Republican presidents.

Source: https://www.usatoday.com/story/news/world/2018/01/19/trumps-foreign-policy-often-put-america-first-and-alone/1036558001/

From withdrawing out of International Trade Agreements, issuing travel bans on people from Muslim-majority countries, building a wall along the U.S. Southern border, attacking the North Atlantic Treaty Organization (NATO) and its U.S. ally countries, separating parents and children of immigrants and asylum seekers at the U.S. border with Mexico regardless of whether they entered legally or not, the way citizens of the international community view America is rapidly changing.

Today, the press in America is being called the "enemy of the people", and accused of producing "fake news", developments which have shaken the nation's core values and principles and sowed seeds of doubt in the populace about the credibility of its previously trusted informers.

It is hoped, however, that the foundation values of this nation which have existed over three centuries and which have made the U.S. a beacon of envy the world over, will prevail over this temporary shift in the character and power dynamics of those empowered to represent the people, and once again propel its people to unlimited horizons of greatness, togetherness, and diversity.

A successful America and its people will not depend on the fear of globalization, fear of immigrants seeking refuge and opportunity in the United States, or fear of the dark vision that the media, international community, asylum seekers, and global partnerships are enemies of the United States .

The future, according to Ian Bremmer (President of Eurasia Group and author of "US vs Them: The Failure of Globalism") and Joe Kennedy III (U.S. Representative from Massachusetts Fourth Congressional District), lies in an active American electorate, fully engaged in its foreign policy and walking hand in hand with the domestic agenda of promoting democracy, individual freedom, human dignity, climate change awareness and reducing carbon emissions in the atmosphere.

Peaceful resolution of conflicts instead of taking up arms, and ensuring that Americans have access to good jobs, healthcare, education, and safety guarantees at home and abroad is another model that will ensure posterity of the people in this country.

Source: https://www.foreignaffairs.com/articles/2018-04-30/time-new-us-foreign-policy-narrative

GREAT SEAL OF THE UNITED STATES

EPILOGUE

After reading this book, I hope you know more about United States of America. For those of you who call this country home, as well as for those visiting this great nation, I hope this has provided you with some of the important things you'll need to take away during your stay.

America Simplified: What You Need to Know cannot contain everything about the United States of America because it would be impossible to downsize all the knowledge, resources, and treasures that the country has acquired over the past three centuries into just one book.

However, the chapters and topics dealt with in this book, I believe, have equipped you or are going to equip you with the tools you need to be a better citizen and an informed man or woman.

There are many things I am sure you will do after reading and understanding this book. For example, you might decide to go on a country-wide tour to see all the places mentioned in this book. You are now in a better position to determine where you might want to live or in which city or state to study. With the knowledge and information from this book, you can hold a successful debate or discussion with your peers about the state of affairs in the United States and point out which areas you want to focus on in the career you decide to take. You can even brag to your friends about the innovations and inventions that America is known for and probably come up with your own invention in the not-so-distant future.

You can say that after reading this book you are never going to be the same again. You are a different you and certainly a better person or citizen, more patriotic, more informed, and aware of the current trends in U.S. life, be it in the social or political arena.

When U.S. citizens travel abroad and interact with children and people from different walks of life, they are surprised to see how much these people know not only about the state of affairs in their home country, but also about world affairs—a stark contrast to what happens in the inland cities, towns, and states in the U.S.

Hopefully, this book will drastically reduce the information gap existing among children, students, and citizens of America and make them more aware of their surroundings and inquisitive enough to keep digging for more.

Below is the list of sources that have been vital to compiling this book. Much appreciation goes to the websites that allow the free use of their photos for such a cause. Without this initiative on their part, it would be difficult to pass credible, vital information onto students and visitors without the visual impression of certain material that calls for it.

BIBLIOGRAPHY

CHAPTER ONE

- http://www.freeworldmaps.net
- https://en.wikipedia.org/wiki/Geography_of_the_United_States
- https://en.wikipedia.org/wiki/The_Star-Spangled_Banner
- https://www.loc.gov/resource/ihas.100010134.0/?sp=2
- https://en.wikipedia.org/wiki/Francis_Scott_Key
- https://images.pexels.com/photos/457563/pexels-photo-457563.jpeg?auto=compress&cs=tinysrgb&dpr=2&h=650&w=940
- https://www.britannica.com/topic/flag-of-the-United-States-of-America
- http://www.usflag.org/colors.html
- https://en.wikipedia.org/wiki/Flag_of_the_United_States,
- http://www.usflag.org/history/flagevolution.html,
- https://hottestheadsofstate.com/us-presidents/
- http://eaglenature.com/eagle_facts.php,
- http://www.adfg.alaska.gov/index.cfm?adfg=baldeagle.main
- https://www.whitehouse.gov/about-the-white-house/the-executive-branch/
- https://en.wikipedia.org/wiki/United_States_dollar

CHAPTER TWO

- https://www.historyisfun.org/pdf/tea-overboard/Why_were_the_American_colonies_unhappy_with_the_British_government.pdf
- http://www.history.org/almanack/life/politics/4thjuly.cfm

- https://www.history.com/this-day-in-history/american-colonies-declare-independence
- https://commons.wikimedia.org/wiki/File:Seal_of_Alabama.svg
- https://upload.wikimedia.org/wikipedia/commons/thumb/e/e6/Flag_of_Alaska.svg/1600px-Flag_of_Alaska.svg.png
- https://en.wikipedia.org/wiki/File:2008_AZ_Proof.png
- https://statesymbolsusa.org/symbol-official-item/arkansas/state-flag/flag-arkansas
- https://flic.kr/p/7kxcQC
- https://commons.wikimedia.org/wiki/File:Flag_of_Colorado_designed_by_Andrew_Carlisle_Carson.svg
- https://statesymbolsusa.org/symbol-official-item/connecticut/state-flag/flag-connecticut
- https://statesymbolsusa.org/symbol-official-item/delaware/state-name-origin/origin-delaware
- https://statesymbolsusa.org/symbol-official-item/florida/state-food-agriculture-symbol/orange-juice
- https://statesymbolsusa.org/symbol-official-item/georgia/state-food-agriculture-symbol/peanut
- https://flic.kr/p/5DyGJv
- https://statesymbolsusa.org/symbol-official-item/illinois/state-seal/seal-illinois
- https://statesymbolsusa.org/symbol-official-item/indiana/state-flag/flag-indiana
- https://en.wikipedia.org/wiki/File:Flag_of_Iowa.svg
- https://en.wikipedia.org/wiki/File:Seal_of_Kansas.svg
- https://statesymbolsusa.org/symbol-official-item/kentucky/cultural-ethnic-org-state-cultural-heritage/kentucky-center-african
- https://commons.wikimedia.org/wiki/File:Seal_of_Louisiana.svg
- https://statesymbolsusa.org/symbol-official-item/maryland/state-name-origin/origin-maryland

- https://en.wikipedia.org/wiki/File:Flag_of_Massachusetts.svg
- https://en.wikipedia.org/wiki/File:2004_MI_Proof.png
- https://statesymbolsusa.org/symbol-official-item/minnesota/state-nickname-state-quarter/north-star-state
- https://flic.kr/p/oTSCsz

CHAPTER THREE

- https://flic.kr/p/p4nAZN
- https://en.wikipedia.org/wiki/File:ChestnutSilver.jpg
- https://en.wikipedia.org/wiki/File:AmericanFoxhound2.jpg
- https://statesymbolsusa.org/symbol/washington/state-seal/seal-washington
- https://en.wikipedia.org/wiki/File:Rhododendron_maximum.jpg
- https://statesymbolsusa.org/symbol/wisconsin/state-fish/muskellunge
- https://flic.kr/p/nW7Sba
- https://state.1keydata.com/state-mottos.php
- https://www.legendsofamerica.com/ah-arksuperstitionmountains/
- https://www.legendsofamerica.com/ca-deathvalley/
- https://www.legendsofamerica.com/ca-lost49ers/
- https://www.independent.co.uk/travel/news-and-advice/weather-heatwave-latest-hottest-places-on-earth-death-valley-aziziyah-dallol-wadi-halfa-lut-desert-a7802366.html
- https://www.cntraveler.com/galleries/2015-11-27/the-hottest-places-in-the-world,
- https://www.livescience.com/19700-hottest-place-earth.html
- https://www.legendsofamerica.com/co-riderdesert/
- https://www.legendsofamerica.com/wy-yellowstonetragedy/
- https://www.legendsofamerica.com/na-crow/
- https://www.legendsofamerica.com/we-overlandtrail/

CHAPTER FOUR

- https://en.wikipedia.org/wiki/Missouri#mediaviewer/File:Flag_of_Missouri.svg
- https://commons.wikimedia.org/wiki/File:Flag_of_Montana.svg
- https://flic.kr/p/geMQJ
- https://commons.wikimedia.org/wiki/File:Flag_of_Nevada.svg
- https://statesymbolsusa.org/sites/statesymbolsusa.org/files/primary-images/NewHampshire-quarterNH.jpg
- https://commons.wikimedia.org/wiki/File:Seal_of_New_Jersey.svg
- https://commons.wikimedia.org/wiki/File:Seal_of_New_York.svg
- https://flic.kr/p/fTgdyT
- https://statesymbolsusa.org/symbol-official-item/north-dakota/state-fish-aquatic-life/northern-pike
- https://flic.kr/p/pGbya8
- https://flic.kr/p/4QSjVr
- https://flic.kr/p/9xqvpU
- https://statesymbolsusa.org/symbol-official-item/pennsylvania/vessels-aircraft/piper-j-3-cub
- https://flic.kr/p/pJgbcY
- https://commons.wikimedia.org/wiki/File:Flag_of_South_Carolina.svg
- https://statesymbolsusa.org/symbol-official-item/south-dakota/state-flag/flag-south-dakota
- https://flic.kr/p/KsenK
- https://statesymbolsusa.org/symbol-official-item/texas/state-food-agriculture-symbol/pan-de-campo
- http://www.worldometers.info/world-population/population-by-country/
- https://census.gov/en.html , http://worldpopulationreview.com/countries/

CHAPTER FIVE

- https://www.usnews.com/news/best-states/rankings/quality-of-life
- https://pixabay.com/photo-3105058/
- https://pixabay.com/en/sheep-mountains-norway-landscape-3744175/
- https://pixabay.com/en/lake-lucerne-region-fountain-3723559/
- https://pixabay.com/en/finnish-oak-island-restaurant-knipan-3454898/
- https://cdn.pixabay.com/photo/2016/06/26/21/38/tram-1481395_1280.jpg
- https://www.usnews.com/news/best-countries/articles/methodology
- https://www.cnbc.com/2018/01/27/us-news-world-report-10-countries-with-the-best-quality-of-life.html
- https://www.usnews.com/news/best-countries/overall-full-list#
- https://www.economist.com/united-states/2018/01/04/life-expectancy-in-america-has-declined-for-two-years-in-a-row
- https://www.cdc.gov/nchs/data/hus/hus17.pdf#highlights
- http://apps.who.int/gho/data/node.main.688?lang=en

CHAPTER SIX

- johngarzon.com
- dunnedwards.com
- https://free-images.com/lg/0b45/lytham_hall_lytham_saint.jpg

CHAPTER SIX

- https://www.census.gov/newsroom/blogs/random-samplings/2017/09/inside_the_american.html

- https://www.usconstitution.net/consttop_lang.html
- https://en.wikipedia.org/wiki/Languages_of_the_United_States
- https://en.wikipedia.org/wiki/Languages_of_the_United_States
- https://statisticalatlas.com/United-States/Languages
- https://en.wikipedia.org/wiki/Religion_in_the_United_States
- https://www.livescience.com/28945-american-culture.html
- https://recipes.howstuffworks.com/menus/5-influences-on-regional-cooking.htm
- https://en.wikipedia.org/wiki/Music_history_of_the_United_States
- https://www.lovehappensmag.com/blog/top-50-fashion-designers/
- https://www.billboard.com/articles/events/greatest-of-all-time/6760872/billboard-greatest-of-all-time-charts-top-songs-album-acts
- https://webvisible.com/hottest-female-singers-id=2665/
- https://www.ranker.com/crowdranked-list/the-25-sexiest-women-in-pop-music
- https://www.selectusa.gov/media-entertainment-industry-united-states
- https://en.wikipedia.org/wiki/List_of_years_in_television
- https://en.wikipedia.org/wiki/History_of_sports_in_the_United_States
- https://www.marintheatre.org/productions/fetch-clay-make-man/fcmm-boxing https://en.wikipedia.org/wiki/Boxing_in_the_United_States

CHAPTER SEVEN

- https://upload.wikimedia.org/wikipedia/commons/4/41/Fly_geyser.jpg
- https://en.wikipedia.org/wiki/The_Wave,_Arizona

- https://cdn.pixabay.com/photo/2012/12/09/05/09/alaska-69135_1280.jpg)
- https://www.world-of-waterfalls.com/images/Horsetail_Falls_13_ns_016L.jpg
- Photo courtesy of Julie and Johnny
- https://www.nps.gov/seki/planyourvisit/sequoiagroves.htm
- https://upload.wikimedia.org/wikipedia/commons/5/57/Great_Lakes_from_space_crop_labeled.jpg
- pexels.com

CHAPTER EIGHT

- http://www.bu.edu/academics/eng/programs/doctoral-programs-overview/
- (www.topuniversities.com

CHAPTER NINE

- https://cdn.pixabay.com/photo/2016/08/02/13/18/combine-harvester-1563394_1280.jpg
- https://upload.wikimedia.org/wikipedia/commons/f/fc/Ibanez_Studio_ST-370_electric_guitar_body.jpg
- https://images.pexels.com/photos/80455/delta-wings-aircraft-stealth-bomber-cloak-of-invisibility-80455.jpeg?auto=compress&cs=tinysrgb&dpr=2&h=350
- https://cdn.pixabay.com/photo/2016/10/25/04/13/jetliner-1767861__480.jpg
- http://history-computer.com/ModernComputer/Personal/Kenbak-1.html
- https://en.wikipedia.org/wiki/Kenbak-1
- https://cdn.pixabay.com/photo/2018/10/29/12/22/motorola-talkr-walk-n-talk-3781021__480.jpg

CHAPTER NINE

- https://upload.wikimedia.org/wikipedia/commons/thumb/a/a1/F-117_Nighthawk_Front.jpg/1599px-F-117_Nighthawk_Front.jpg
- https://www.usg.edu/galileo/skills/unit07/internet07_02.phtml
- https://en.wikipedia.org/wiki/ARPANET , https://en.wikipedia.org/wiki/Internet
- https://en.wikipedia.org/wiki/Timeline_of_United_States_inventions
- https://en.wikipedia.org/wiki/Timeline_of_United_States_inventions_(1890–1945)
- https://en.wikipedia.org/wiki/Timeline_of_United_States_inventions_(1946–91)
- https://en.wikipedia.org/wiki/Timeline_of_United_States_inventions_(after_1991)
- https://www.uspto.gov/about-us/news-updates/united-states-issues-patent-number-10000000

CHAPTER TEN

- https://www.worldatlas.com/articles/biggest-heists-and-bank-robberies-in-american-history.html

CHAPTER ELEVEN

- https://geology.com/world/world-map-clickable.gif
- https://images.pexels.com/photos/853168/pexels-photo-853168.jpeg?auto=compress&cs=tinysrgb&dpr=2&h=650&w=940
- https://image.shutterstock.com/image-photo/los-angeles-feb-10-jennifer-450w-136598402.jpg
- https://image.shutterstock.com/image-photo/venice-italy-august-31-lady-450w-1196414656.jpg

- https://image.shutterstock.com/image-photo/r-kelly-performs-on-stage-450w-546085786.jpg
- https://image.shutterstock.com/image-photo/las-vegas-may-20-taylor-450w-1097570879.jpg
- https://image.shutterstock.com/image-photo/los-angeles-feb-10-faith-450w-1129097489.jpg
- https://image.shutterstock.com/image-photo/ariana-grande-2016-american-music-450w-522342139.jpg
- https://image.shutterstock.com/image-photo/los-angeles-feb-10-beyonce-450w-1129097909.jpg

CHAPTER ELEVEN

- https://image.shutterstock.com/z/stock-photo-kanye-west-and-jay-z-at-the-world-premiere-of-jay-z-s-fade-to-black-at-the-the-ziegfeld-theater-on-160850204.jpg
- https://image.shutterstock.com/image-photo/cannes-france-may-11-justin-450w-732211825.jpg
- https://www.boxofficemojo.com/alltime/world/
- https://www.newsday.com/entertainment/movies/the-biggest-box-office-hits-of-all-time-1.5369007
- https://www.filmsite.org/boxoffice.html
- : http://time.com/money/5095574/the-10-richest-people-in-america/
- https://www.forbes.com/forbes-400/#577d19257e2f
- http://time.com/money/5096770/richest-women-in-america/
- https://www.forbes.com/profile/evan-spiegel/?list=forbes-400#1dd1ffb5529c
- https://www.forbes.com/profile/bobby-murphy/?list=forbes-400#3763784b37ba
- http://www.crf-usa.org/war-in-iraq/foreign-policy.html

- https://www.usatoday.com/story/news/world/2018/01/19/trumps-foreign-policy-often-put-america-first-and-alone/1036558001/
- https://www.foreignaffairs.com/articles/2018-04-30/time-new-us-foreign-policy-narrative

Michael Ntabaazi is a Journalist by training and a past-time broadcast and print journalist. He studied journalism in Uganda, Kenya, South Africa, and Germany.

He has previously worked and practiced in the above countries. Michael is very inquisitive and passionate about people.

This is Michael Ntabaazi's first book as he seeks to explore uncharted waters in a new field of interest just beginning to unfold.

He lives in Massachusetts, U.S.A.

www.ingramcontent.com/pod-product-compliance
Lightning Source LLC
Chambersburg PA
CBHW041221270326
41932CB00006B/46